The Almaniac

A woman's guide t...

HA·HA·UCK

GUILTY

Written and illustrated by
Sue Ingleton

For Sylvia —
with love Suzanne.

ALLEN & UNWIN

First published 1990
Allen & Unwin Australia Pty Ltd
8 Napier Street, North Sydney NSW 2059 Australia

National Library of Australia
Cataloguing-in-Publication entry:

Ingleton, Sue.
Sue Ingleton's Almaniac.

ISBN 0 04 920105 0.

1. Home economics — Humor. 2. Housewives — Humor.
I. Title. II. Title: Almaniac, a woman's guide to
domestic insanity

640.207

Library of Congress Catalog Card Number: 90-053307

Set in 11/12pt Goudy Old Style by Excel Imaging
Printed by Australian Print Group, Maryborough, Vic.

INTRODUCTION

The **Almaniac** is a haphazard guide to a year—any year that you happen to buy this book—even better if someone has given it you, it is only after all, what is known in the trade as a 'stocking filler' (and now you know how important you are to the person who thrust this on you).

Please do not try to read this book all at once. You will tire very quickly of the humour and will lose the desired impact—*just **one** laugh a day keeps the psychiatrist away.*

'Housewives should not try to laugh more than once a day, they could lose their sense of humour.' *S. Freud*

It's true some weeks are missing, in fact there may even be times when some months are missing; you know what it's like though, those times when one week just seems like the last and you can't even remember living through June. It's a bit like driving the kids to school every day down the same road. You leave the house and you get home and you can't even remember having dropped them off let alone driving home; you can't even remember their names sometimes.

Whatever happens though, the **Almaniac** will put its finger on it for you. Within these pages lies the solutions to all your problems. You may not like the solution, you may not even understand it, but be assured that if you follow the advice given here you will surely change the face of domestic womanhood by the end of the year!

This book is dedicated to my three people
Dylan, Maudie and Roxane.

January 1, New Year's Day

Book of the Week
Dale Spender *Women of Ideas*

Advice for the Day

A New Year and an Old You!
Last night may have been a disappointing non-event for
some. Never mind. Today is a good day to forget the
past and look forward to the rest of your life. What
you make of it will provide a source of continual
argument both for you, your loved ones and your bank
manager.
It is usual for most people to look ahead to a New
Year through bloodshot eyes, but you, being a fully
cognisant housewife (having stayed sober so that
someone could drive home last night) can see perfectly
clearly the looming awfulness of it all. This year
though, you have a secret weapon! The *Almaniac*.
Careful consultation will guarantee you a successful
twelve months of auspicious home management and
controllable domestic insanity.

Things to Avoid

Dependance on Almanacs. All methods of divination
are susceptible to errors. Nothing is ever guaranteed in
the Universe.

Quote of the Day
Harmony exists in difference no less than in likeness.

Margaret Fuller, 1843

January 2

Advice for the Day

Today is a good day to stay in bed, put Blue Tack in
your ears and let everyone start the week without you.
Assure them that you will soon catch up.

Things to Avoid

Opening mail.
Don't go near any water, unless you are submerging
your whole body in the medium. Just remember to
keep breathing. Tomorrow, as the poets say, is another
day.

Quote of the Day

Cinderella and the prince
lived, they say, happily ever after,
like two dolls in a museum case
never bothered by diapers or dust,
never arguing over the timing of an egg,
never telling the same story twice,
never getting a middle-aged spread.

Anne Sexton

January 3

Advice for the Day

Three days into the new year and already you feel like
packing it in. This is quite normal considering what
you have to put up with. Take heart from the
knowledge that at least two million other women out
there are having the same depression, for the same
reasons :

- The overpriced toy you bought your youngest child
  has disintegrated in the bath. He demands that
  Father Christmas replace it immediately;
- The book shop refuses to exchange the ten books
  you were given for Christmas, all of which you
  already had (and hadn't even enjoyed reading once,
  let alone twice);
- The kids are totally hyper having devoured all the
  Chocolate Money, Father Christmases, Lady Beetles,
  Irish Liqueurs, Cherry Liqueurs et al and are
  refusing to eat any more turkey 'anythings'!

Things to Avoid

Not a good day to look closely at the people you have
brought into this world, at least not until you submit
and take them to McDonalds, whereupon they will
transform into cherubs. Fast food does have its
advantages.

Quote of the Day

We have to recognise, at this moment of history, as
through centuries past, that most of our sons are—in the
most profound sense—virtually fatherless.

Adrienne Rich

January 4

Advice for the Day

It's a good day for food preparation, especially propitious to cook your favourite meal despite the fact that no one else in the house can stand it. You will find that, for once, you will just smile benignly when they howl you down and just go on shovelling it into your mouth. This behaviour will have them nonplussed and they will be forced to eat Muesli Flakes instead.

Things to Avoid

Don't have any Muesli Flakes in the house.

Quote of the Day

No, the secret of my youthful appearance is simply—
mashed swede. As a face mask, as a night cap, and in an
emergency, as a draught-excluder.
I do have to be careful of my health, because I have a
grumbling ovary which once flared up in the middle of
The Gondoliers.

Victoria Wood

January 5

Advice for the Day

More and more you begin to understand the reason why McDonalds is so popular. When you finally capitulate: 'OK! You can go to McDonalds. (sob),' you see this look of love and adoration, usually reserved for baby guinea pigs, directed at **you**! Mothers just want to be loved, to be made to feel that it's all worthwhile, all the pain and anguish and despair and rejection and guilt and self-hatred and and and . . .

Things to Avoid

On no account eat anything yourself at McDonalds, unless it **is** yourself. You may suck your thumb, bite your nails etc.

Quote of the Day

Equality means men coming up to our standards. It means men meeting our standards of nurturing. It does not mean that we should deny our nurturing, our strength as mothers, to meet theirs!

Dora Russell

January 6

Advice for the Day

Today you will be overtaken by a subconscious desire to seek and destroy. Go with it. It's a valuable asset in any housewife. The *Almaniac* suggests that you concentrate your efforts below the belt. Items to be found: dirty underpants and smelly socks.

Things to Avoid

Avoid any household appliances that require water. If there is anything to be washed it is advised to burn it instead.

Quote of the Day

I did not believe a baby would come out of me. I mean look at what had gone *in*!

Alice Walker

January 7

Advice for the Day

Today is a very auspicious one for standing as an independent candidate for parliament. You will find that your inexhaustible capacity for listening to chatter and squabbling of boys, your inherent capabilities of sound reasoning, your conspicuously exacting handling of home accounts and your overriding, deep emotional security will provide you with all the answers needed to run the country in the manner to which we would like to see it become accustomed.

Things to Avoid

Avoid giving any preferences to party politics.

Quote of the Day

Under the male definition of femininity there is the notion of female 'hairlessness'. The feminine woman has no facial hair, no hair on arms or legs or underarms, and women who wish to conform to this definition of femininity will constantly present themselves to males without a hint of hair.

Dale Spender

January 8

Advice for the Day

Today you will be assailed from many quarters to part with money. None of these omens, such as bills, rates notices, tennis club raffles, hold any lasting threat in them. It will be quite safe to ignore all such portents and continue with your original plans for a personal massage, sauna and akido class.

Things to Avoid

Avoid opening any bank statements. They will only prove detrimental to your plans for the day.

Quote of the Day

Everywhere I go I'm asked if I think universities stifle writers. In my opinion they don't stifle enough of them. There's many a bestseller that could have been prevented by a good teacher.

Flannery O'Connor

January 9

Advice for the Day

Today you may be harassed by door to door salespeople. It's propitious to be acquiescent and agreeable. You never know who you might meet, after all! Sign up for everything, especially the ones where they promise to return in person to follow up their products. You will find that at the end of the day not only will you have increased your list of 'people I know' but you will also have increased your list of 'people I owe' and that's always very satisfying at the end of the month. Remember the more money we owe the more we feel alive!

Things to Avoid

Not a good day to think about other people's needs.

Quote of the Day

The biggest sin is sitting on your arse.

Florynce Kennedy

January 10

Advice for the Day

It's a good day for attending to those small fix-it jobs
which have been piling up over the last lifetime. Your
fingernails, the rough skin on your heels, the tinea
problem. A little TLC in the right places will make a
newish woman of you ...

Things to Avoid

Avoid all contact with mirrors. Sometimes even just
looking in a mirror can add seven years to your life.

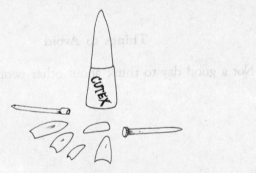

Quote of the Day

The true artist will let his wife slave, his children go
barefoot, his mother drudge for him at 70, sooner than
work at anything but his art.

G. B. Shaw

A true artist is her own wife, her children are always
cared for, she does her own drudging and her art
becomes everything she touches.

Ingleton

January 11

Advice for the Day

It's very helpful as a New Age Housewife to be in touch with the cosmos and to come to a deeper understanding of why all these terrible things keep happening to you and how you can avoid them. Learning to throw the I Ching is the first step on the path of enlightenment. You may purchase this book at your favourite New Age shop. To throw the I Ching does take a little practice but the best method is usually to just pick it up and aim it at the head of the person who is giving you the shits.

Things to Avoid

Not a good day to let your tenosynovitis get the best of you.

Quote of the Day

Women need not always keep their mouths shut and their wombs open.

Emma Goldman

January 12

Beds play a large part in the stars for today. You will
have trouble getting out of them and there may be
even more pressure, once you're out, to get back in.
This could come from an unexpected source so—be on
your toes!

Things to Avoid

Avoid eating corn chips, biscuits or toast for breakfast.

Quote of the Day

'Do not put such unlimited power in the hands of
husbands. Remember all men would be tyrants if they
could.'

Abigail Adams

*a plea to her husband John Adams who was drawing up
the Constitution of the United States 1777. He ignored it.*

January 13

Advice for the Day

It seems that the pressure is on to get that fabulous
body of yours out into the open, competing in
marathon running! Marathon running is the boon of
the modern housewife and the **Almaniac** recommends
solid workouts to prepare you for the big event which
this year could see you winning. No more 'first *woman*'
over the line crap, you will be the first *person* over the
line. Some housewives find that to have the kids, pets
and husband in back of them is more conducive to
keeping the pace up. Others, who are usually in
therapy, find they need the whole family out in front,
just out of earshot as it were, luring them on.
Whatever you choose let them know you need them
there.

Things to Avoid

Avoid heavy intakes of fluid before the race, you know
how your waterworks are subject to premature
ejaculation since the last birth, and remember, if your
period is due, don't hold it in! Let it flow! You may
win on a sympathy vote when they see you pounding
down to the finish line with blood-soaked Reeboks.

Quote of the Day

You know what they call a woman who uses the rhythm
method? Mother.

Kathy Lette

January 14

Advice for the Day

Today is a good day for going to the chemist. You will
find that he will renew all your out-of-date
prescriptions for valium, tryptanol and librium without
so much as a how-do-you-do-it.

Things to Avoid

Avoid reading *How To Heal Your Life* by Louise Hay.

Quote of the Day

The pills are a mother, but better,
every color and as good as sour balls.
I'm on a diet from death.

Anne Sexton

January 15–21

Book of the Week

Harriet Martineau *Harriet Martineau On Women*

Advice for the Week

A week set aside to recover from Christmas and New Year and to immerse yourself in the January sales. Take down the Christmas tree, January sales, clean all the fake snow off the windows, January sales, find the old chocolate Christmas decorations that the mice have removed and stashed in the piano, January sales. A general clean up this week and a firm resolution not to be here next Christmas nor to spend any money unless it's at the January sales.

Things to Avoid

Avoid personal contact with your bank manager.

Quote of the Week

But through centuries of suckling men emotionally at our breasts we have also been told that we were polluted, devouring, domineering, masochistic, harpies, bitches, dykes and whores.
We are slowly learning to discredit these recitals, including the one that begins, 'Mothers are more real than other women'.

Adrienne Rich

January 22

Book of the Week

Charlotte Bronte Villette

Advice for the Day

Recreation of various kinds will present itself to you today. People will want you to make a four at tennis, people will want you to make a four at bridge, but no one will offer you foreplay—never mind. It's best to refuse all offers. Biblical references will help you get over any embarrassment and if they know you're an atheist plead menstrual contusions and vitamin deficiencies.

Things to Avoid

Avoid moving too fast today, you may fall over.

Quote of the Day

Before marriage a man will lie awake thinking about something you said; after marriage, he'll fall asleep before you finish saying it.

Helen Rowland

January 23

Advice for the Day

Today is a good day for indulging the children. Cook three pots full of spaghetti bolognaise and insist that they can eat it at every meal—breakfast as well. If they refuse, they must watch television between the hours of noon to 3pm and 7pm onwards including all the news and current affairs programs. In Sweden this is called Tel/Aversion Therapy.

Things to Avoid

Avoid all wholefoods, brown rice and green vegetables for 24 hours.

Quote of the Day

If a man is highly sexed he's virile. If a woman is, she's a nymphomaniac. With them it's power but with us it's a disease! Even the act of sex is called penetration! Why don't they call it enclosure?

Gemma Hatchback

January 24

Advice for the Day

Today will be one of those days where you just won't
be able to sit down. It could mean that your furniture
has been repossessed or that the paint just isn't dry
from yesterday's bout of home renovation. Don't panic.
There's always the gravity boots. Sling yourself up and
out of harm's way.

Things to Avoid

Not a good day to pay any attention to your varicose
veins.

Quote of the Day

Long before I knew her [Dorothy Parker] she dined in
Paris with a group of lesbians who were seriously talking
of the possibility of legal marriage between them. Dottie
listened most politely, clucked in agreement. They
expected her friendly opinion and asked for it. The eyes
large with sympathy, 'Of course you must have legal
marriages. There are the children to be considered.'

Lillian Hellman

January 25

Advice for the Day

If ill health has been plaguing you today is a good day
to visit the medical profession to complain about the
treatment that's been causing all your problems. Take a
copy of *Our Bodies, Ourselves* and refer to it
constantly, stopping the medico the minute they try to
put over their 'mystification of medicine' on you.

Things to Avoid

Avoid all advice that begins with 'I know exactly how
you feel . . .'

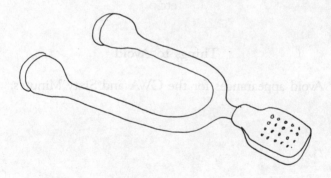

Quote of the Day

If women are supposed to be less rational and more
emotional at the beginning of our menstrual cycle when
the female hormone is at its lowest level then why isn't it
logical to say that, in those few days, women behave the
most like the way men behave all month long?

Gloria Steinem

January 26

Advice for the Day

The New Age has truly sucked you in (you should worry when you feel it has sucked you off). Channelling is all the go. And it's all so terribly simple. Those voices you hear in your head at the oddest moments—making sandwiches, changing nappies, making nappies, changing sandwiches ... You become aware of a higher power. Just lie down, relax and *let* the voice come through.

There's a lot of money to be made from channelling today. You may charge up to $50 a head. It doesn't matter what you say and even better if you don't remember afterwards. Pretty soon you can graduate to private functions, twenty-first birthdays, bar mitzvahs etc.

Things to Avoid

Avoid appearances for the CWA and Sixty Minutes.

Quote of the Day

Mama. Mama, do you understand
Why I've not bound myself to a man?
Is there something buried in your old widow's mind
That blesses my choice of our own kind?
Oh Mama, Mama.

Meg Christian

January 27

Advice for the Day

Any minute now the kids will be back at school and you can resume your normal life of smoking drugs, painting your toenails, watching the soaps, eating Mars Bars and generally having the good time that they don't know about.

Things to Avoid

When the kids get home it is not a good idea to be in the same chair you were in when they left for school.

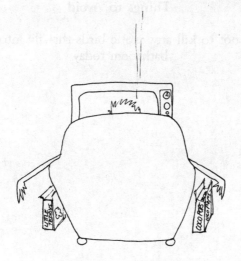

Quote of the Day

Until we can see what we are we cannot take steps to become what we should be.

Charlotte Perkins Gilman, 1898

January 28

Advice for the Day

Could be one of those days when your 'ex' calls to say
he is going to sail up the Amazon for two months with
his new girlfriend who is an ornithologist even though
she's only eighteen, and that means that he won't be
able to take the kids on alternate weekends for the
next six months because they're coming home via a
trip to Europe. Little things like this are sent to try us.
Keep a gay outlook on life and join the Lesbian
Mothers' Club immediately.

Things to Avoid

Try not to kill any exotic birds that fly into the
bathroom today.

Quote of the Day

The most exhausting thing in life is being insincere.

Anne Morrow Lindbergh

January 29

Advice for the Day

A day relaxing in the garden would be auspicious. If
you don't have a garden then sit on the pot plants, if
you don't have pot plants ... well, no wonder you are
so screwed up. Surround yourself immediately with
growing things that only require water, a little seaweed
and gentle thoughts. It makes such a change from the
'growing' things that you are usually supporting.

Things to Avoid

Avoid giving 'Grow-Plus' to the kids and 'Dynamic
Lifter' to the husband. They will neither be accepted
nor have the required effect.

Quote of the Day

... our blood flows and we extend ourselves without ever
reaching an end; we never hold back our thoughts, our
signs, our writing; and we're not afraid of lacking.

Hélène Cixous

January 30

Advice for the Day

Today you will find your bodily functions will demand
a lot from you. Go with it. If you're menstruating then
let the blood run free. Remember it's only your magic
blood, neither is it dangerous nor unhygienic. It's
strange to note that in all those war movies that men
keep making the copious quantities of blood just
bucket out, splash on buddies, soak through fatigues,
smear on faces and generally fill up the screen. But put
a drop of the blood of life in there, as opposed to the
blood of death and Wow! Just watch them run!
Disgusting!
Bleed on the seagrass matting, on the lino, on the
futon. It's your day. As the poets say: Don't suture the
day !

Things to Avoid

Avoid all products that have 'for your protection'
written on them.

Quote of the Day

Thou shalt not rape was conspicuously missing from the
Ten Commandments.

Susan Brownmiller

January 31

Magic spells day

Spell for attracting Money from Zsuzsanna Budapest

Must be a Waxing Moon. Out of green cloth fashion a
doll with eyes, mouth and nose of red thread. Stuff it
with eucalyptus leaves. Imagine it is you. When the
new moon is in the sky light two green candles and
burn your favourite incense. Pass the doll through the
smoke saying 'I name you [your name]. You are
Success! You are powerful! You will always have more
than enough!' Sprinkle it with gold glitter and call in
the amount you need. Don't be over-extravagant. Say 'I
conjure the spirits who guard the wealth of this earth
to bless me with wealth'. Kiss it and lick it. 'I call on
the waters to bless my spell with love.'
Wrap it in a white cloth and hide it in a dark
womblike place. Repeat this spell *nine* nights in a row;
on the tenth night, make a permanent hiding place for
it and don't forget to burn it after you get the money.

Quote of the Day

Marriage is as certain bane to love as lending money is to
friendship.

Aphra Behn, 1670

February 1

Advice for the Day

Today is favourable to do some Past Life Recall work.
Tapes for guidance are readily available from your local
New Age Bookshop at an exorbitant price, but then
in the New Age philosophy one shouldn't have to
worry about money. You will get everything you need
just by visualising it ! Visualise yourself owning the
tape and by some strange coincidence it will be in your
coat pocket when you get home. Plug in and start
straight away.

Things to Avoid

Not a good time to let gut feelings of honesty override
your needs.

Quote of the Day

Being pregnant is like having PMT for nine months and
when you finally do have a period it's got arms and legs
and a head and you've got to look after it for at least ten
years!

Gemma Hatchback

February 2

Advice for the Day

Today you may find that you are living in the past.
This could be due to the fact that you are now
inhabiting another's body and forgot to turn off the
tape yesterday.

Things to Avoid

Avoid leaving your body before the kids have gone to
school.

Quote of the Day

The freedom of women from sex oppression either
matters or it does not; it is either essential or it is not.
Decide one more time.

Andrea Dworkin

February 3

Advice for the Day

It could be Saturday. One of those days when the cries of 'I'm bored' will drive you bananas. Let it. Throw bananas at everyone, eat them, mash them up and use them as a face mask. The sight of you covered in bananas will soon shut them up. There's nothing like a bout of hysteria to frighten children into submission.

Things to Avoid

Avoid becoming truly hysterical, it could upset your evening meditation on the banana lounge.

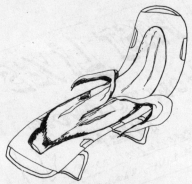

Quote of the Day

What a denial of our humanity that at the centres of power, where decisions are made, there is no room for nurturing, for love, and children. There is more to life than the 'inhuman' workplace. It is terrible that many men do not know that: it is a tragedy if women follow them.

Dora Russell

February 4

Book of the Week

Rebecca West *The Fountain Overflows*.

Advice for the Day

A very creative day for you today. Go to the video shop and get out 'The Exterminator'. Watch it carefully, noting the misogyny of the plot line and rewrite the dialogue to turn it into a comedy. Submit your script to the Women's Film Fund or the Defence Department.

Things to Avoid

Avoid becoming emotionally involved in men's bodies and their misuse of them.

Quote of the Day

You'd better change your ways
And get really wild
I want to tell you something
I wouldn't tell you no lie.
Wild women are the only kind
That really get by,
'Cause Wild Women don't worry
Wild Women don't get the blues.

Ida Cox

February 5

Advice for the Day

You become acutely aware of menstruation today.
Perhaps you're in for a day of heavy bleeding or
perhaps you overheard your daughter talking about 'the
curse' and, as most of us do, you wince at this awful
reference. Take the time to explain to her (and
yourself) the true meaning of 'the curse.' *See below*.
Acknowledge that it is not a denigratory term but in
fact is a term of female power. A curse sealed with
menstrual blood could not be broken.

Things to Avoid

Avoid watching television ads that associate
menstruation with white doves, daisies and billowing
ballgowns.

Quote of the Day

The terrible vehicle of the feminine curse was the
menstrual blood, still called *The Curse*. To 'damn' has
been linked with the Hebrew dam, 'blood', specifically
mother-blood, the fluid of the womb, anciently thought
to create one's very soul—and destroy it.

Barbara Walker

February 6

Advice for the Day

Bringing up children in the isolation of the suburban dream, or in the overcrowded environment of high rise council flats or in the opulence of your condominium ... it's all the same! Ghastly. Decide now that the answer is to have a full time surrogate mother, a British nanny, an au pair girl, an Indian ayah! Go to the CES immediately and put in your order. You will be amazed at the tiny amount of interest that is shown in this 'fulfilling and fascinating' job. Perhaps you have to offer the same salary as the chief executive of BHP: then you might get someone dedicated enough to put up with motherhood seven days a week, but don't expect Robert Holmes à Court to apply.

Things to Avoid

Not a good day to think about your monetary worth on the labour exchange.

Quote of the Day

No coward soul is mine. No trembler in the world's storm-troubled sphere.

Emily Bronte

February 7

Advice for the Day

Contraception could be rearing it's ugly head again. It is amazing to realise that in this day and age we still don't control our own bodies. You will notice that whenever women seem to be getting the upper hand in society there will be some male parliamentarian who will demand a tighter control over women's bodies on the pretext that they care about life. These are usually the same politicians who vote for increases in defence spending. Go to the demos and keep writing letters.

Things to Avoid

Avoid IUDs. Their only useful purpose is as jewellery. IUD earrings are a party stopper.

Quote of the Day

Women learn to believe no longer in what men say when they exalt woman or exalt man: the one thing they are sure of is this rifled and bleeding womb, these shreds of crimson life, this child that is not there. It is at her first abortion that woman begins to 'know'.

Simone de Beauvoir

February 8

Advice for the Day

Sleep, that blessed state of oblivion, has been evading you for the past few weeks. When you find yourself blearily leaning over to cut up your husband's meal into small, bite-size chunks; when you stack the Weetbix carefully into the refrigerator and put the milk in the pantry; when you find yourself ironing teatowels—you know that the cogs have stopped turning. Go to bed immediately with a pillow strapped around your brain.

Things to Avoid

Do not leave the telephone plugged in.

Quote of the Day

I am trying with all my skill to do a painting that is all of woman, as well as all of me.

Georgia O'Keefe

February 9

Advice for the Day

Lucky stars continue to shine on anyone who is
travelling or buying livestock. What a strange
prediction for one as domestic as you! The stars also
say it is a safe time to be doing things with water. Put
those two together and it means you can race out and
buy that new puppy, it is guaranteed that it will only
shit on the lino and not on the carpet.

Things to Avoid

Don't wear that brand new outfit today or at any time
in the future while you have livestock in the house.

Quote of the Day

This work [*The First Sex*] is the result of the convergence
of two streams of thought: the first, that the earliest
civilization we know was but a renewal of a then dimly
remembered and now utterly forgotten older one; and the
second, that the impelling and revivifying agent in what
we know as civilization was woman.

Elizabeth Gould Davis

February 10

Advice for the Day

According to the **Almaniac** this is a good day on which to give your house a thorough spring clean.

Things to Avoid

This is not a good day for reading the **Almaniac**.

Quote of the Day

We have a long history of men sacrificing their children with impunity in the name of various causes, for religion, for war, or even for family honour. But if a woman—who gave them life—takes it away, it becomes a horror story, not a glorious state.

Dora Russell

February 11–17

Book of the Week

Diane Bell *Daughters of the Dreaming*

Advice for the Week

This week looks like being a big no-no. School sports, parent/teacher nights, student strikes, postal strikes, transport strikes. Let's forget it and hold our breath 'til next week. However do not neglect your brain: keep reading.

Things to Avoid

Avoid putting yourself up for fund raising committees—the temptation to fiddle the books will be too strong for you in this month of penury.

Quote of the Week

I don't want to say I'm getting attached to my vibrator, but last Valentine's Day I sent it two dozen roses.

Robin Tyler

February 18

Advice for the Day

It's too early in the year to be thinking about suicide
... and anyway school has only just started and you
haven't finished making that sports uniform yet so your
daughter would never forgive you if you did yourself in
right now and your mother would not understand and
blame herself and your husband would probably end
up with that dreadful girl in the typing pool and
everyone would be tramping through the house and it's
in such a mess that you'd have to do a thorough
spring clean before you killed yourself so you might as
well live. It's less exhausting.

Things to Avoid

Sylvia Plath's poetry.

Quote of the Day

When men go away, the women instantly create a kind of
hedonistic, permissive, indulgent world where they try on
dresses, cook, gossip and have a lovely time—it's a relief
from the rigours of the world where they have to do so
much boring hard work. An archetypal male world is
militaristic, hierarchic, disciplinary, often humourless.

Doris Lessing

February 19

Information Day

Midwifery

Medieval Christianity detested midwives for their
connections with pagan matriarchy Goddess-worship.
Churchmen viewed them as implacable enemies of the
Catholic faith. Handbooks of the Inquisition stated:
'No one does more harm to the Catholic faith than
midwives'. The real reason for ecclesiastical hostility
seems to have been the notion that midwives could
help women control their own fate, learn secrets of sex
and birth control, or procure abortions. The pagan
women of antiquity had considerable knowledge of
such matters, which was considered women's own
business, not subject to male authority.

Toward the end of the nineteenth century, male
doctors moved in on the last remaining area of
exclusively female medicine, and took the midwifery-
trade away from women. At the instigation of the
American Medical Association, the US Congress
outlawed midwives, and the new male 'obstetricians'
replaced them.

Barbara Walker

Disinformation
Pregnancy is a 'medical problem'.

Quote of the Day
A man's home is his castle.

Anon

A man's home is a hassle.

Ingleton

February 20

Advice for the Day

If the little ones are driving you round the bend put
them all in the car and drive them round the bend, to
the auto car wash. Lock them in the car, slip the
attendant $40 and tell him to keep running it through
till you get back. Abscond to the nearest feminist
bookshop and spend the afternoon just browsing.

Things to Avoid

Don't get sidetracked into Safeways thinking you
should do the shopping as well.

Quote of the Day

The pride of women will never be laid in the dust.

Gaelic proverb

February 21

Advice for the Day

A good day to get into the garden and dig up the bones of all those ex-husbands that are stopping the fruit trees from growing.

Things to Avoid

This is a bad time to begin a period of mourning. Be sure to inform your friends and relatives that they are not to do anything untoward and if they do, not to let you know until the end of next week.

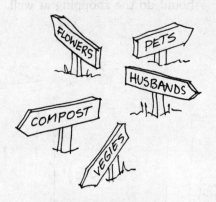

Quote of the Day

If a man yells 'woman driver' at me, he is not telling me that I am a woman. 'Woman' does not refer to me, it refers to my driving ... in his mind bad driving is an attribute of women. It's precisely that connotative use of 'woman' which I object to when you talk about women doctors, women politicians, and so on.

Alicia Lee

February 22

Advice for the Day

Another day for gardening. Yesterday was very
productive but today you may have a few setbacks.
One being that wherever you plunge your green little
fingers into the garden you are met with the smell of
stale urine, stale *male* urine—it has a distinctive quality.
Why is it that men feel the necessity to pull their
dicks out and piss all over everything? Is it because
they never think of weeding the garden or is it that
they, like dogs, need to mark out their territory?
Complain, and if it still happens take to squatting on
the bonnet of his car. Do it all over his gumboots, piss
on his Black and Decker, make small puddles on the
form guide . . .

Things to Avoid

The joy of pissing in the open air could become
addictive. Avoid squatting in the supermarket
carpark—a man would not get arrested but you would.

Quote of the Day

We women are always in danger of living too exclusively
in the affections; and though our affections are perhaps
the best gifts we have, we ought also to have our share of
the more independent life.

George Eliot

February 23

Advice for the Day

Back to nature has become a driving passion in your life. The 'primitive' really begins to appeal to you. Your bodily functions are to be expressed openly, after all nature made you beautiful. Wearing skirts without any undies has become the order of the day. You can piss in the Botanical Gardens without anybody even realising what you're doing down there. Menstruation is not a problem, you stay home for five days and just bleed into the grass: this is what they used to do in tribal communities. You also get off doing any work with this attitude.

Things to Avoid

Avoid overdosing on Vitamin 'C'. It turns your urine bright yellow, thereby making it more noticeable against the white marble of the steps of Parliament House.

Quote of the Day

I never have much use for a man although they do come in handy when one wants to move a piano.

Rebecca West

February 24

Advice for the Day

Although the **Almaniac** is highly qualified in the areas of sexual advice you will find that less and less it wants to talk about it. This is probably due to the fact that there are now millions of books and videos doing the job quite successfully. The information is there, you just have to go out and buy it. If you are having trouble here's what to do: always go to your Mother first. Her advice will be useless but you will make her feel so good that you have come to her first with your sexual problems that you may even heal the gaping wounds between you. The next person to consult is your local librarian. She will be so amazed at this affront to your privacy that you may just change her life. And so it goes ... your sexual problems will heal the world ... eventually ...

Things to Avoid

Confiding in men.

Quote of the Day

Take back your gold and give me current love,
The treasure of your heart, not of your purse.

Aphra Behn, 1686

February 25–March 10, Two Weeks

Books for the Weeks

Joy Williams *Breaking and Entering*
Mary Webb *Precious Bane*

Vipassana is an intensive meditation course where you keep still and look at your pain but are not allowed to mention it to anyone else. They wouldn't want to listen anyway, since they are suffering the same, if not more than you. Two weeks of silence and screaming internally can do wonders for the soul. These next two weeks you are advised to take Vipassana. You are reminded to read your books before you go, as you are not allowed to take any reading matter with you (it might take your mind off the pain).
At the end of these two weeks you will be qualified to talk about pain to practically everyone.

Things to Avoid

Avoid telling your friends about the pain. Keep it a big secret but by all means encourage them to take Vipassana.

Quote of the Weeks

Cunt is not a slang, dialect or any marginal form, but a true language word, and of the oldest stock. Derivative of the Oriental Great Goddess Cunti, the Yoni of the Universe. "Cunctipotent", all powerful (i.e. having cunt magic), also cunning, kenning, and ken: knowledge, learning, insight, remembrance, wisdom.

Barbara Walker

March 11

Nawal El Saadawi *Woman At Point Zero*

Advice for the Day

Other people's problems loom large.
- You could be asked to drive an old lady to hospital, just because you backed over her in the carpark;
- Your friend's child chokes on your vibrator and has to be rushed to the clinic;
- Your neighbour's lawyer has sent you a threatening letter about the blue gum that fell on their barbeque last Sunday and maimed two High Court judges.

Things to Avoid

Do not run away. Do not buy another ticket in Lotto.

Quote of the Day

Woman must learn that her freedom will reach as far as her power to achieve her freedom reaches.

Emma Goldman

March 12

Advice for the Day

Those lawyer's letters just keep coming from:
- The woman whose little boy was bitten by your sister's dog whilst she was holidaying in Vanuatu and you were doing the right thing and taking the vicious monster for walkies;
- The shopkeeper whose wire door was demolished by your sister's dog as the adoring animal tried to keep you in his sight;
- Your sister, who refuses to take any responsibility for the behaviour of an animal that was in your care.

Things to Avoid

Murdering dogs or sisters.

Quote of the Day

The devil's in her tongue, and so 'tis in most women's of her age; for when it has quitted the tail, it repairs to the upper tire.

Aphra Behn

March 13

Advice for the Day

A day of bad timing. You finally meet the mother of
the monstrous child who has been causing all that pain
to your little one at school. You cannot contain
yourself. You go up to her, and without saying anything
you sock her in the mouth. It's only as she is
staggering to her feet that you realise not only is she
slightly retarded (even more so now) but she is
pregnant as well . . .

Things to Avoid

Not a good day to become emotionally involved in
other people's personality defects, even if they are your
own children.

Quote of the Day

As long as women sit and feel sorry for themselves in
their isolation whilst their men go out at night and go
out to work and in fact leave home at every moment to
seek a wider and richer life, so long as women are willing
to accept this, so long will they stay at home.

Hephzibah Menuhin

March 14

Advice for the Day

Balls loom large on the agenda today. Normally this
could be quite an exciting prediction, but no.
- Could be your netball team has given you the push.
  You are not dedicated enough it seems and also you
  refused to go to the Hen's Night male strip show
  which has really put their collective nose out of
  joint;
- You may be hit on the breast by a volley ball, an
  innocent bystander at the school sports, maimed
  and crippled. You may never breastfeed again;
- You accidentally elbow the cute guy at touch
  football in his privates and he swears off the game
  forever, never to return.

Things to Avoid

Avoid going into litigation over personal injuries
whether to your body or your ego.

Quote of the Day

The greatest enemy of any enlightened society, and
especially of women, is the organised clergy.

Shulamit Aloni

March 15

Advice for the Day

Revolutionise the tuckshop today. Have a mild attack of hysteria making sure you crush underfoot the 100 loaves of sliced white; in passing, pull the cord out of the deep freeze and melt the icy poles. Surreptitiously stack the Mars Bars in the oven and toss the sausage rolls and chicken nuggets down the insinkerator. At 11.45 am when panic sets in calmly announce that you've got 100 loaves of kibble rye, three cartons of carob cookies, rennet-free cheese by the kilo and fresh fruit and veg all in the back of your station wagon.

Things to Avoid

Avoid being there when the kids arrive for their lunches.

Quote of the Day

This cathexis between mother and daughter—essential, distorted, misused—is the great unwritten story. Probably there is nothing in human nature more resonant with charges than the flow of energy between two biologically alike bodies, one of which has lain in amniotic bliss inside the other, one of which has laboured to give birth to the other.

Adrienne Rich

March 16

Advice for the Day

Beneficial to lie on beaches today, yours or someone else's, it doesn't matter which. Your carcinomas may be feeling neglected—show them that you really care and give yourself about five hours in the sun with only Plus 4 blockout.

Things to Avoid

Not a good day for long term health problems.

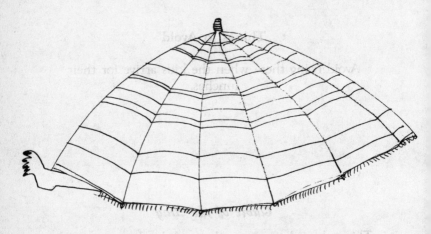

Quote of the Day

Have you noticed how doctors and prostitutes both use a red light to show where they're operating? The big difference is that the prostitute uses *her* body to make money and the doctor uses *yours!*

Gemma Hatchback

March 17

Advice for the Day

A good day at the supermarket to remind your
favourite check-out girl not to lean her ovaries over the
electronic counter. Produce copious figures
documenting the hundreds of miscarriages, spontaneous
abortions and cancers that have erupted due to being
in close proximity to the electrons pouring out of
these man-made wonders.

Things to Avoid

Supermarket managers.

Quote of the Day

Reverse everything. Make women the point of departure
in judging, make darkness the point of departure in
judging what men call light, make obscurity the point of
departure in judging what men call clarity . . .

Marguerite Duras

March 18

Advice for the Day

You will be invited to a school chums' reunion. Accept
and send your mother in your place. Tell her not to let
on that she is not you. It will make all those women
feel so good that they haven't aged as much as they
thought they had.

Things to Avoid

Not a good day to contemplate that you are becoming
just like your mother.

Quote of the Day

There are few traumas greater . . . than the wife's
discovery of her husband's dependencies; than the
discovery of her own gut-superiority in a thousand hidden
crannies of their relationship; than the realization that in
many situations his judgement is no better than hers; that
he does not really know more than she; that he is not
the calm, rational, non-emotional dealer in facts and
relevant arguments; that he is, in brief, not at all the kind
of person the male stereotype pictures him to be. Equally,
if not more serious, is her recognition that she is not
really the weaker vessel, that she is often called upon to
be the strong one in the relationship.

Jessie Bernard

March 19

Diane Stein *The Women's Spirituality Book*

Advice for the Day

A good day to be selfish and attend to your needs.
Remember the words of Matilda Joselyn Gage: 'the
male doctrine of Christianity was based upon the
conception that woman had no right to live for herself
alone. Her duty to others has continuously been placed
before her and her training has ever been that of
self-sacrifice' (1892). No more self sacrifice; *you* eat the
last steak in the fridge, *you* take the front seat on the Big
Dipper, *you* lick the beaters!

Things To Avoid

Don't lick the beaters if they are still in the mixmaster
and plugged in. Your kids could take a nasty revenge.

Quote of the Day

If men could get pregnant, abortion would be a
sacrament.

Irish NY Taxi Driver (female) to Florynce Kennedy

March 20

Advice for the Day

Financial pressures mean you have to take a fifth job. The stars say that you can squeeze it in between the hours of 2 to 4am. Prostitution is the obvious answer. It is advised that you learn to astral travel before picking up this option of relieving the pressure from the bank manager. (However *he* could well be your first client, if you play your cards right. Just tell him to take it off the mortgage principal.)

Things to Avoid

Not a good day to see the film 'Broken Mirrors' by Marlene Gorris.

Quote of the Day

Most women are one man away from welfare.

quoted to Gloria Steinem

March 21

Advice for the Day

If tradesmen bend your ear today about how their wives don't understand them, be sympathetic and commiserate. A nice stance is the Sybil Fawlty one of just leaning and saying 'I knowwww'. After they've gone on for long enough begin to tell them how awful *your* wife is. This will confuse them initially until they finally twig that you must be one of those 'lebanese wimmin'. Correct the mistake for them, 'no, *les*bian women'. Thus you will be assured of a deliciously entertaining afternoon as you observe the male of the species assert and justify his existence.

Things to Avoid

Tradeswomen who complain about their wives.

Quote of the Day

We are contrary to men because they are contrary to that which is good.

Jane Anger, 1589

March 22

An invitation from the View Club could disrupt your plans for the week, especially since they are asking you to talk on the subject of 'How To Keep A Good Man Down'. Never having had a good man you feel rather unqualified to talk on the subject. You could suggest to them that you are very well qualified to talk about 'How to Pretend That the Boy You Married Will One Day Be a Man'.

Things to Avoid

Avoid reading your essay to your husband for syntax corrections.

Quote of the Day

If there is to be any romance in marriage woman must be given every chance to earn a decent living at other occupations. Otherwise no man can be sure that he is loved for himself alone, and that his wife did not come to the Registry Office because she had no luck at the Labour Exchange.

Rebecca West

March 23

Advice for the Day

Although the Ides of March were last week you have these weird, almost Shakespearean feelings of betrayal looming in the wings. Watch your back, say the stars. Wearing three bras will give you a feeling of added protection to the chest area and using garlic oil instead of your usual musk oil will give you heaps of psychic protection and ensure that people don't get too close. Betrayal on a domestic level can be very destructive. Just the fact that your local healthfood shop forgot to put aside your order for tempeh can give you a severe attack of personal-regressive-negativity.

Things to Avoid

Avoid saying to yourself 'people just don't like me'.

Quote of the Day

I'm tough. I wear my stilettos inside out.

Sheila Shit

March 24

Advice for the Day

Children's birthdays are becoming more and more complicated. Unless you just opt to dump them all at McDonalds, you have to be prepared to entertain and gratify the most excessive of imaginations. Force feeding them is one solution to while away the three odd hours. Calculate around a dozen party pies per mouth. Make a birthday cake in the shape of an entire football team, or if he's a boy, the complete Bolshoi Ballet doing Coppelia; offer prizes—usually money is the most effective—for whoever eats the most food. Borrow three television sets and VCRs from friends and put a stack of videos beside each, giving them the entire range 'Disney', 'Elm Street', 'Omen', 'White Christmas' etc.
Retire to the patio with a G&T and your Walkman.

Things to Avoid

Try not to have more than one birthday party per week.

Quote of the Day

Men have felt it necessary to isolate themselves from women, from human creation, from the rhythms of life and the feelings of nurturance, so that they can protect themselves and their pursuit of pure reason. And this is the basis of their education system.

Dora Russell

March 25

Advice for the Day

One of those days when the peculiar smell coming
from the refrigerator reminds you that you haven't
delved into it's lower reaches for at least two months.
Take today off and strip the refrigerator! Wear your
bathers, bring in the hose and have yourself some fun.
After all it's *your* fridge. At the end of the day,
hopefully, nothing will have survived your manic
onslaught. You will be left with a pure, pristine, clean
and totally empty fridge. Await the cries of despair
when they troop in after school and open its door.
They will utter (in the same tone as they use when the
fridge is stacked full) 'There's nothing to eat in here!'
Smile gracefully and say 'It's really the only way I can
keep it clean' and go to bed.

Things to Avoid

Don't let them know you have a supply of food under
your bed.

Quote of the Day

As a woman, I have no country. As a woman I want no
country. As a woman my country is the whole world.

Virginia Woolf

March 26

Kate Chopin *The Awakening*

Advice for the Day

The unseasonal weather will play havoc with your new interest in Japanese food. Nori will go mouldy, moths run rampant in the soba and the hijiki goes soft and smells like it might be dangerous. How do the Japanese cope you ask yourself? Well they don't. That's why so many of them are trying to live on a time-share basis in Australia. They even go to Australian cooking classes before they embark on their holidays (which are simply a front to acclimatise them for permanent settlement here). Our solution is to quit buying overpriced Japanese products, eat Australian raw fish, seaweed available at all beaches, and talk a lot to Japanese tourists about the Greenhouse effect and how it destroys sushi.

Things to Avoid

All seaweed from all beaches where there are hypodermic syringes in the sand.

Quote of the Day

The women of today are the thoughts of their mothers and grandmothers, embodied, and made alive. They are active, capable, determined and bound to win. They have one thousand generations back of them ... Millions of women, dead and gone, are speaking through us today.

Matilda Joselyn Gage, 1892

March 27

Advice for the Day

A good day for losing weight. How to lose 5 kilos in five minutes? Chop a leg off! Ho ho. No, relax, there are other ways. The simplest way is to stop swallowing. You can eat whatever you like just don't swallow it! Of course it can be most unattractive but we're sure you will devise clever little ways to spit your food into glad bags (for the dog) unnoticed. At restaurants you can be more open about it. Just remember 'The Meaning of Life' and call for an ice bucket. After the meal don't neglect to send your compliments to the chef. Also, now you can boast that not only do you take the kids to McDonalds but **you** eat there as well!

Things to Avoid

McDonalds. If you have to go there, don't let the kids swallow their food.

Quote of the Day

Women must come off the pedestal. Men put us up there to get us out of the way.

Viscountess Rhondda

March 28

Advice for the Day

If you are reading your book, as you should be, you will gradually begin to understand that centuries of suppression of female sexuality and emotions have generated enormous internal pressures which are expressed in male violence against women and have evolved the stereotypical degrading label of the 'emotional and irrational' woman and 'the humourless feminist'. Aaaargh!

Try to remain emotional and irrational especially once you understand the standards against which you are measured.

Things to Avoid

Avoid getting too involved in semantics today.
It's OK to scream a lot.

Quote of the Day

My mother adorned with flowers whatever shabby house we were forced to live in. Whatever she planted grew as if by magic ... Because of her creativity with her flowers, even my memories of poverty are seen through a screen of blooms—sunflowers, petunias, roses, dahlias, forsythia, spirea, delphiniums, verbena ... and on and on.

Alice Walker

March 29, Good Friday

Advice for the Day

Crucifixion for some but not for you! Anyway there's always something inherently good about Friday. The first holiday you've scored all year so make the most of it. Have about 10 dozen packets of hot cross buns in the kitchen, enough to last all weekend and stay in bed. Put the TV and VCR in your room, lock the door and watch Scorsese's 'The Last Temptation Of Christ'. It's OK to demand a hot cup of tea and a hot bun, every now and then, but hold the vinegar.

Things to Avoid

Avoid all buns in the oven.

Quote of the Day

Easter was a Springtime sacrificial festival showing its Pagan origin in a dating system based on the old lunar calendar. The Easter Bunny was older than Christianity; it was the Moon-hare sacred to the Goddess Eostre in both eastern and western nations. People exchanged eggs, the symbol of life and rebirth.

Barbara Walker

March 30, Easter Saturday

Advice for the Day

By now the family has got used to your incapacitation which you have named a 'Return to the Tomb.' You will find that they will all leave home and go round to Grandma's for meals. Make sure you have arranged for Grandma to be in hospital having her veins done.

Things to Avoid

Not a good day to be planning a new family, even if the old one gives you the shits.

Quote of the Day

Parliament is a man's game. It's a substitute for civil war and duelling. It's based completely on the idea of *conflict*. You have to be party *adversaries*. There has to be *opposition*. If one party chooses one thing in its platform, the other party has to show it's different, it has to oppose it. Have you ever heard of anything so ridiculous?

Dora Russell

March 31, Easter Sunday

Advice for the Day

Tell the kids that somewhere 'out there' are hidden
300 Easter Eggs of varying sizes and at least 100 have
Smarties inside them. Since you have in fact only
bought three eggs and hidden them in fairly obvious
places the kids will spend all day out there, lured by
their easy find of the morning. Assure them that, like
Jesus, you will rise again.

Things to Avoid

Avoid getting involved in any arguments about crosses
to bear.

Quote of the Day

Snow White, the dumb bunny,
opened the door
and she bit into a poison apple
and fell down for the final time.

Anne Sexton

April 1, April Fools Day

'Love makes fools of us all.' A celebration peculiar to women, venerating the Goddess of Love, sensuality and outrageous behaviour! In ancient Rome the women ordered their lovers on senseless errands in proof of their love and devotion. Later on women's sexuality was to be belittled and made fun of, thereby minimalising its power.

Advice for the Day

Such a good day to play jokes. The night before, organise for your best friend to ring up about 7am. Make sure you answer the phone. A look of horror creeps over your face as you say 'yes, yes, oh dear, alright'. Turn to the kids and say 'My God, your school burnt down last night!' Just give them long enough to plan their next few months of unexpected holidays and then turn on them and say 'April Fool!' Ho ho, will you be popular!

Things to Avoid

Do not turn your back on anyone under fifteen till noon.

Quote of the Day

Until I was twenty-one I measured my orgasms against Lady Chatterley's and wondered what was *wrong* with me. Did it ever occur to me that Lady Chatterley was really a man? That she was really D. H. Lawrence?

Erica Jong

April 2–8

Ann J. Lane *The Charlotte Perkins Gilman Reader*

Advice for the Week

No predictions this week.
Sometimes even the stars just couldn't care; and
anyway you shouldn't spend all your time reading
Almanacs. You are behind on your reading list and you
must have picked up from the first three months that
this book would have to be the most unreliable guide
to living in the nineties that has ever been published.
Get cracking on that list, it's *your* life you're trying to
change!

Things to Avoid

Since the stars are refusing to cooperate perhaps you
could just try avoiding anything that smacks of the
metaphysical e.g. final payment notices from Telecom.

The face to us in sleep is beautiful. The small body lying
against our body vulnerable. The cries move us. Secretly
we remove the child's clothing, the blanket, the diaper.
We fondle the body. We love this body, because we are
part of the body. We are mothers.

Susan Grifffin

April 9

Zora Neale Hurston *And Their Eyes Were Watching God*

Advice for the Day

Safe to do washing today. You will find yourself asking why the male of the species have such huge skid marks on their undies. Don't they know where their arseholes are? Let's face it, they've only got one hole down there and they can't even find it.

Things to Avoid

Not a good day to ask for foreplay if it involves finding your clitoris (and if it doesn't please write to the author revealing your own methods, for future reference).

Quote of the Day

Is man only a blunder of God or God only a blunder of man?

F. Nietzsche

Right both times Fred.

Ingleton

April 10

Advice for the Day

A good day for flying interstate, or intestate (don't
make a will before you fly, it shows a distinct lack of
faith in the Goddess), however there's nothing to stop
you using your inheritance to get away. A quick round
trip, a short stopover in an airport bar, scintillating
conversation with a femocrat, a whole new existence
and then be back in time for tea.

Things to Avoid

Avoid having conversations with air hostesses about the
regularity of their periods.

Quote of the Day

You stay young as long as you can learn, acquire new
habits and suffer contradiction.

Marie von Ebner-Eschenbach

April 11

Advice for the Day

A day for shopping in the panic that surrounds the
general public every time a long weekend comes up.
What is it about them? They are instilled with
consumer rash. They buy copious amounts of food,
more than they will ever need for a week let alone
four days. And all this is for a holiday that celebrates a
Springtime Festival and here we are at the end of
Autumn going into Winter! Make a protest. No one
will understand what you're talking about but you will
secure your growing reputation as a Lunatic Housewife.
This is always helpful for future assaults on the system.

Things to Avoid

Do not attack the easter bunny in the supermarket
and if possible demand to sit on its knee and have
your photo taken.

Quote of the Day

The silence in women is such that anything that falls into
it has an enormous reverberation. Whereas in men, this
silence no longer exists . . .

Marguerite Duras

April 12, Magic Spells Day

PROTECTIVE CIRCLE

*To be used on your car when you park it; for your house
when you leave it unattended; use it on your loved ones
as they set off on a journey
without you etc.*

Visualise a circle of white light with the energy
spinning around in the direction of the sun (in
Australia that's anti-clockwise!) Visualise casting a
pentacle of white light over doors, windows etc.

Say: Pentacle of white light
Keep——safe, bound tight
In protective love and light.

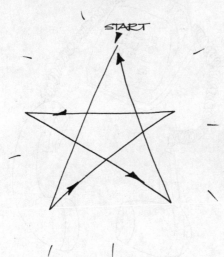

START

Quote of the Day

Woman will always be dependant until she holds a purse
of her own.

Elizabeth Cady Stanton

April 13

Advice for the Day

The stars today will come into conjunction and thereby
render all micro-wave appliances powerless. This is
therefore the only time it is safe to stand in front of
your microwave oven for long periods without your
protective lead-lined apron on.

Things to Avoid

Never go near a microwave while it is waving.

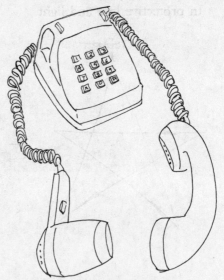

Quote of the Day

Wit has truth in it; wisecracking is simply calisthenics
with words.

Dorothy Parker

April 14

Advice for the Day

As there are about only 260 shopping days to Christmas it is advisable to start buying immediately. This way by the time you come to wrap up their presents you will ensure yourself a really good time. Each little item will have been long forgotten and this means you will almost have as much fun as the kids, especially when you realise that everything has gone up at least 30% since you bought it.

Things to Avoid

Avoid forgetting where your stash place is.

Quote of the Day

I'm extremely happy living by myself and solitude is my favourite thing.

Doris Lessing

April 15

Advice for the Day

Life will deal you a lucky hand today, if not yours,
then someone else's. Just make sure you put it to good
use and find your 'G' spot asap.

Things to Avoid

Avoid whatever turns you off.

Quote of the Day

Sisterhood, like female friendship, has as its core the
affirmation of freedom. Thus sisterhood differs radically
from male comradeship/brotherhood, which functions to
perpetuate the State of War.

Mary Daly

April 16

Tillie Olsen *Mother to Daughter Daughter to Mother*

Advice for the Day

Instead of spending your household budget on
clothing, petrol and food, save it up for a few months
(David Suzuki is right, we are far too greedy and
wasteful) and invest it in a second-hand Macintosh
Plus. We assume the *Almaniac* is not being read by
poor people, but if you *are* poor remember: with
careful scrimping and saving, your Family Allowance
cheques *do* make a difference. Once you get hooked
into your computer you won't notice that the kids are
starving and in rags and that you never go out any
more. You will write five novels within the first month,
none of which will be rejected by publishers if you
sign them with interesting names like Helen Garner,
Elizabeth Jolley, Princess Margaret etc.

Things to Avoid

Not a good idea to use your real name, ever, on a
manuscript.

Quote of the Day

When the short skirt came in it was a step in the right
direction of freedom; for it gave women a freer use of
their legs than they had known for hundreds of years.
Incidentally it gave them back the use of the left hand
which in the days of trailing skirts had to be used for
holding the ugly things up out of the dust and dirt.

Crystal Eastman

April 17

Advice for the Day

Your children are complaining of being beaten up at school. You decide you must make them self-sufficient in the area of violence. Steel capped boots, boxing, karate and chemical warfare all present themselves as viable options. Then you hear about passive resistance but that smacks of subservience (to the untrained mind) and that dreadful film on Ghandi, so you reject it. Then you hear about magic. This appeals to the witch in you and you proceed immediately to read up on it and teach the kids!

Things to Avoid

Not a good time yet to tell the kids what you are planning. Say you are writing letters to the editor, that always impresses.

Quote of the Day

The witch was in reality the profoundest thinker, the most advanced scientist of those ages . . . As knowledge has ever been power, the church feared its use in women's hands and levelled their deadliest blows at her.

Matilda Joselyn Gage, 1892

April 18

Advice for the Day

New Age technology is all the rage this week. It is a
good time to buy crystal. Not the German sort, but
the simple quartz variety. Remember the rules: you must
choose the crystal that *chooses* you. This may sound
hard when they're all just staring at you from their
glass cases in your favourite NA shop but do not be
depressed. The choice is usually very easy. Most people
find that the crystal that chooses them is usually the
cheapest one there. Concentrate on the cheapest one.

Things to Avoid

Not a good day to take your Bankcard.

Quote of the Day

Obvious and inexorable oppression that cannot be
overcome does not give rise to revolt but to submission.

Simone Weil

April 19

Advice for the Day

A good day for making deals and swapping chores.
Ring up a friend and tell her you'll do her toilets this
week if she'll do yours. Cleaning up someone else's
shit always has an air of indecency about it. Good for
the hidden voyeur in you. Make sure you give your
toilets a quick going over before your friend arrives;
you don't want her to think you are a slut.

Things to Avoid

Avoid all cleaning agents that are bio-degradable. It's
degrading enough to have clean toilets as it is.

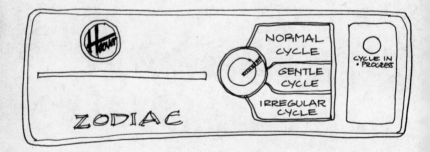

Quote of the Day

Boys will be boys but girls will be women.

Feminist graffiti

April 20

Advice for the Day

Mutilation is the order of the day. Decide on a new
look you. Have your ears pierced all the way around
and be a 'with-it mum'. Get the chemist to stick ring
pulls from beer cans in them. You will cause a minor
sensation when you pick up the kids from school.

Things to Avoid

Parent/teacher meetings.

Quote of the Day

She was a widow of sixty then. She'd had her feet bound
when she was about five. I asked her if it had hurt. 'I
have never in all the years that have passed forgotten the
pain ... for a long time both feet were like lumps of
burning coal. I couldn't bear to put a blanket over them
even in the coldest weather. For years I cried all night.'
This woman had never been given a name other than
little sister. When she married she was the wife and
daughter-in-law of so-and-so, and when she had a child
she was the mother of so-and-so. She didn't exist as an
individual.

Dymphna Cusack

April 21

Advice for the Day

Stocktaking Day today. Have fun:
- Search out all those tomato sauce bottles and pour them into one huge bottle and chain it to the sideboard;
- Attack the liquor cupboard and tip all those small amounts of gin, vodka, whisky etc. into one bottle, write MINE on it and proceed to drink it when 'himself' wanders in after a hard day at his orifice;
- Gather together all the single socks and stick them on the picket fence outside your house. It makes an attractive display, especially in winter when the garden is devoid of blooms.

Things to Avoid

Not advisable to sit down in the banana lounge at any time today.

Quote of the Day

In male culture, police are heroic and so are outlaws ... the conflicts between these groups embody the male commitment to violence ... It is a mistake to view the warring factions of male culture as genuinely distinct from one another: in fact, these warring factions operate in near-perfect harmony to keep women at their mercy, one way or another.

Andrea Dworkin

April 22

Advice for the Day

This could be a day of natural disasters in the home.
The washing machine will overload and pour thirty
gallons of water through the house. Never mind. Turn
it to your advantage. If you can't claim on the
insurance squeeze a couple of bottles of Sunlight liquid
over the floor and invite your children's friends over to
play rugby inside. You will find you have accomplished
a full spring clean. Pray for hot weather tomorrow.

Things to Avoid

On the other hand forget about the Sunlight liquid,
we feel you may be pouring good money after bad.

Quote of the Day

... once, when I was a young lady and on a night
express ... I was awakened by a man coming in from the
corridor and taking hold of my leg ... Quite as much to
my own astonishment as his, I uttered the most appalling
growl that ever came out of a tigress. He fled, poor man,
without a word: and I lay there, trembling slightly, not at
my escape but at my potentialities.

Sylvia Townsend Warner

April 23

Monique Wittig *The Opopomax*

Advice for the Day

Someone has reported you to the Welfare department. It must be the ring pulls in your ears that has set them off. Go with it. Let them take the kids away. You deserve a break every now and then. Have the pulls surgically removed and wrap your ears in comfrey compresses and when they are healed you can go and demand your children back.

Things to Avoid

Avoid telling your husband where they have gone (the children, not the ring pulls). He might not understand.

Quote of the Day

Enjoy that time of the month —
put a battery in your tampon!

Sheila Shit

April 24

Advice for the Day

Well, tomorrow is Anzac Day. You spend the day
painting your placards and slogans and teeing up your
demo positions with your local 'Reclaim The Night
Group' and 'Women Against Rape'.

Things to Avoid

Do not make banners out of destructible material.
Soak all banners with itching powder before you leave
in the morning for the dawn vigil.

Quote of the Day

A chant is taught to the GI recruits when they're in
basic training:
>   This is my weapon (you point to your rifle)
>   This is my gun (and you point to your penis)
>   This is for business (that's the rifle)
>   And this is for fun ..

Susan Brownmiller

April 25, Anzac Day

Advice for the Day

Today is a good day to get out and protest! There will
be many causes which you may choose to support.
Remember—for the most impact in a protest you just
have to keep laughing. This will not be hard when you
are confronted with the sight of so many men dressed
up in ribbons and jewellery celebrating death and rape.

Things to Avoid

Not a good day to get serious about anything.
Remember not to touch the banners.

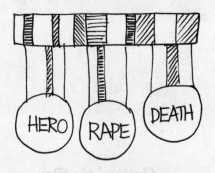

Quote of the Day

Anzac Day is not only about mourning. It's a massive
celebration of masculinity—dead and living. Australia is
unique in defining it's national identity through the
celebration of a resounding defeat, at Gallipoli.

Rosemary Pringle

April 26

Advice for the Day

The best solution for an attack of itching powder is to
stay under water all day. Spend the day in the bath
reminiscing how wonderful it was when the old
General fell off his horse as he tried to run you over.

Things to Avoid

Don't answer the phone and only do television
interviews.

Quote of the Day

I objected that the girls (prostitutes) were picked up by
the police but never the men. Soldiers got off scot-free
because it was wartime and the judge said 'Miss Cusack,
if you say things like that I'll have you up for contempt
of court' and I said, 'Your honour, that's exactly what I
feel'.

Dymphna Cusack

April 27

Advice for the Day

Not paying all those parking fines has finally caught up
with you. An unattractive specimen of the 'boys in
blue' presents you with your marching orders. Go to
Jail, move directly to Jail, do not pass water etc. etc.
Take the monopoly set with you, it'll help pass time,
also your reading matter and journal. Look at this
positively. It's a chance to get out of the house for a
few days, you've saved a lot of money and the
experience will be invaluable when you write your
memoirs. Look at what it did for Oscar Wilde and
Lindy Chamberlain.

Things to Avoid

Self-recrimination. This is after all your Karma.

Quote of the Day

There is no way that woman, with her power to vote will
ever purify politics.

Emma Goldman

April 28

Advice for the Day

Being in Jail is proving to be ghastly, this is the reason why not many people that you know go there. You have had very little time for yourself and by the time you want to go to bed and read they turn the lights out. Still, look at the positive side. The food is so lousy you are losing weight. Your new haircut will grow out. The uniform is actually quite cute and you have this wonderful idea to go into the fashion business and start a new punk wave rage of 'Screw You Gear' when you are on the outside.

Things to Avoid

Not a good time to talk up wimmins lib to the inmates.

Quote of the Day

Now you have touched the women,
you have struck the rock,
you have dislodged a boulder,
you will be crushed.

South African Women's Freedom Song

April 29

Advice for the Day

Freedom. Now you really appreciate the joys of modern
living. The right to breathe in lead poisoning, to be hit
by cars on the pedestrian crossing, to be ripped off in
the supermarket. This feeling of euphoria will last
about two hours and then you will have to hold your
press conference.

Things to Avoid

Avoid complaining about prison menus, it makes
taxpayers irate.

Quote of the Day

Let us have wine and women, mirth and laughter
Sermons and soda water the day after.

Byron

Let's have wine and women, mirth and laughter
No farts, halitosis or rough cheeks the morning after.

Ingleton

April 30

Advice for the Day

It's the start of the football season which means that
the cricket season must be finally over. ('Over'. Get it?!)
We must remind ourselves that the Goddess does
provide us with small mercies.

Things to Avoid

Avoid watching television on Saturday and Sunday for
the next six months.

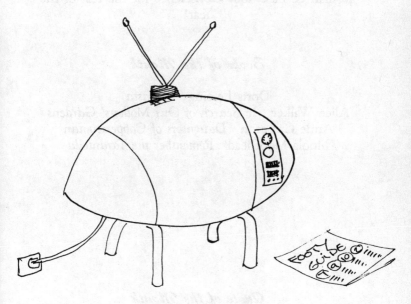

Quote of the Day

Men hate those whom they have hurt.

Harriet Martineau

May

The month of May presents us with very few opportunities to express ourselves; it's nearly winter and the **Almaniac** suggests preparing for hibernation. Skip May and go on to June.

Two events in May to look out for.

The May Day March, which let's face it, you've probably never been to, can be acknowledged from a distance. If you feel the need to attend you could carry a placard saying 'Workers of the World! Who washes your socks?'

Mothers Day, originally Mothering Sunday; now a marketing bonanza: 'Spend up Big on the Little Woman & Ease Your Conscience for the rest of the Year'.

Books of the Month

Doris Lessing *Shikasta*
Alice Walker *In Search of Our Mothers' Gardens*
Anne Cameron *Daughters of Copperwoman*
Finola Moorhead *Remember the Tarantella*

Quote of the Month

The roaring laughter of women is like the roaring of the eternal sea.

Mary Daly

June 1

Book of the Week

Marion Bradley *The Mists of Avalon*

Advice For The Day

Today is a good day to write a novella. Some suggested
titles are: 'How to Refuse to Cook a Meal', 'How to
Stop Pretending You're Wrong When You Know
You're Right'. Of course the only way you would ever
have time to write a book would be to get a grant
from the Literature Board which you would then use
to bribe another woman to look after your kids while
you lock yourself in the bathroom with the Birko and
the word processor.

Things to Avoid

Not a good day to feel guilty about not massaging the
Male Ego.

Quote of the Day

The mother—poor invaded soul—finds even the
bathroom door no bar to hammering hands.

Carlotte Perkins Gilman, 1896

Advice for two Days

You are advised to abscond to a place of rest for *two days*. A friendly lesbian neighbour perhaps or, if that is a bit threatening for you, try the rest room at David Jones. Remember to ring meals-on-wheels and report an invalid (as in 'not valid') man with dependants who will require some attention.

Things to Avoid

Avoid taking nembutal; watch the Midday Show instead.

Quote of the Day

A hag was a woman who would not be wooed by a man. 'Hagiology' means the study of holy matters and saints.

Barbara Walker

June 4

Advice for the Day

Excellent time to enrol in a Women's Health Workshop
(funny how they don't have health workshops for men,
perhaps they don't realise that they are really sick).
Women's Health Workshops are entirely justifiable on
the grounds that everyone *knows* we're really sick. Sick
of this and sick of that! Sick of being called Sex
Objects, especially when we don't object
to sex.

Things to Avoid

Not a good day for looking at the world through clear
glass.

Quote of the Day

We have not outgrown the myth that woman has no soul,
that she is a mere appendage to man, made out of his rib.
Perhaps the poor quality of the material from whence she
came is the reason for her inferiority.

Emma Goldman

June 5

Advice for the Day

Looks like one of those days when you're going to be caught short. As a safeguard it's always been advisable to stash tampons, everywhere. In the sofa, the piano, the deep-freeze, the phone-moneybox, jackets, coats, down umbrellas etc. Your friends will also come to rely on you. Everytime you walk in the door they'll know you've got them covered and they'll breathe a sigh of relief!

Things to Avoid

Avoid adapting to a sea sponge at this time. You could lose a lot of friends; borrowing a tampon is much less personal than borrowing a sea sponge.

Quote of the Day

Oh, little girl,
my stringbean,
how do you grow?
You grow this way.
You are too many to eat.

Anne Sexton

June 6

Advice for the Day

Time to contemplate what it will be like when the children have grown up and you have your divorce. The joys of living alone, or perhaps with a like-minded woman are too numerous to mention. Here are some:

- The toilet seat is always down;
- That pen that you were using is still there after three days;
- There's never any pressure to cook a meal, and you are the last person to insist.

Things to Avoid

You won't have to avoid anything now you're your own woman.

Quote of the Day

I have always thought that every woman should marry, and no man.

B. Disraeli

I have always thought that no woman should marry, and every man should have a valet.

Ingleton

June 7

Advice for the Day

A good day to have lunch with the girls and talk
about your operations. Remember when women talk
about their operations it's only to confirm amongst
themselves the general level of incompetence and
arrogance that afflicts the medical profession.

Things to Avoid

Avoid showing scars in public (emotional or physical)
unless they are man-made.

Quote of the Day

It was bad enough that women might be able to find a
way to defy so-called natural order and have sex without
babies, but what was even worse was that such a
pamphlet (on birth control) might come into the hands of
their wives, who would read the astonishing statement
that it was perfectly reasonable for a woman to expect to
enjoy sexual intercourse. This was a new idea for many
women and it brought with it another one: if they were
not enjoying sex, then what could be wrong with their
husbands? No wonder so many men were intent on
suppressing the pamphlet!

Dora Russell

June 8

Book of the Week

Adrienne Rich *Of Woman Born*

Advice for the Day

If some of your children have left home, gone to college or entered the workforce, don't expect to ever hear from them again, unless they haven't got a tumble dryer.

Things to Avoid

Avoid taking in other people's washing.

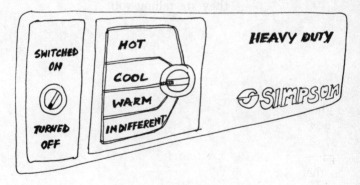

Quote of the Day

How strange and awful it seemed to stand naked under the sky! How delicious! She felt like some newborn creature, opening its eyes in a familiar world that it had never known.

Kate Chopin, 1899

June 9

Advice for the Day

If you have a mind to start renovations today it will be
another nail in the DIY coffin. Tradesmen will fail to
appear in the order which they are needed. The
plasterer turns up but can't start till the electrician,
who hasn't turned up, has finished. Sound advice. Give
him a dozen stubbies and drag as much information
out of him as possible on rendering and float finishes.
By tomorrow you can give him the sack and do it
yourself.

Things to Avoid

Avoid letting tradesmen think you understand what
they are telling you.

Quote of the Day

The basic freedom of the world is women's freedom.

Margaret Sanger

June 10

Advice for the Day

A positive day for meeting and making new friends.
Accept a social invitation, you could be in for a
pleasant surprise. The stars promise you more than a
children's birthday party, but probably less than than a
tupperware party.

Things to Avoid

Not a good day to confront your dark side. Avoid
buying beetroot containers.

Quote of the Day

Elizabeth Cady Stanton was a witty and challenging
speaker. During a stop in Lincoln, Nebraska, a man asked
her 'Don't you think that the best thing a woman can do
is to perform well her part in the role of wife and
mother? My wife has presented me with eight beautiful
sons. Is not that better lifework than that of exercising
the right of suffrage?'
• Stanton surveyed him from head to foot and
answered coolly 'I have met few men worth repeating
eight times'.

Crystal Eastman

June 11

Advice for the Day

If you have time and strength it's a good day to demolish old walls and clear away rubble. Dig up the sewer and unblock the wad of tampons, probably the result of your teenage daughter's weekend pyjama party; if it's not tampons that's doing it it could be three rolls of toilet paper and the teddy bear that your toddler disposed of last week.

Things to Avoid

This is a bad day to start work on that 14 part mini-series for ABC/TV based on the idea of 'Women in Men's Jobs'.

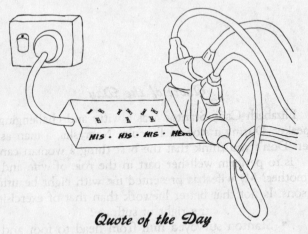

Quote of the Day

Love is the most divine passion of the soul and without it man is both unfinished and unhappy.

Aphra Behn, 1670

June 12

Advice for the Day

Stocktaking Day. Time again to:

- Find all the batteries lying around and by licking the end of them you can find out if they've got any oomph left in them. Your tongue will tingle. You could develop this into a wonderful children's party game and thereby save yourself the trouble of standing round all day licking batteries;
- Rifle drawers and collect all those underpants, put them in a cardboard box with a sign saying: 'Don't ever make me buy you any more underpants for at least ten years, dickhead!'

Things to Avoid

Avoid the temptation to smell any underpants you may find today.

Quote of the Day

I'm tough. I burnt my bra while I was still wearing it.

Sheila Shit

June 13

Advice for the Day

Surround yourself with beautiful things today and just pamper, pamper, pamper. For example: your bank account before you did the Christmas shopping; all those bottles of nailpolish you used to use before you did housework; magazine photos of models who can afford to use skin rejuvenating products (why do they always use twenty year olds to advertise ageing skin?), photos of your children.

Things to Avoid

Don't avoid anything today, whatever you do it's OK.

Quote of the Day

If there is an ass protecting the system, ass-kicking should be undertaken regardless of the sex, ethnicity, or charm of the ass involved.

Florynce Kennedy

June 14

Advice for the Day

Go into publishing; desktop publishing is all the rage. Start a magazine called *Home Ugly*. It could be a best seller. Get your friends to contribute, but only the ones who won't be offended by the title and the fact that you want to feature their kitchens on the front cover.

Things to Avoid

Not a good day to read the Ikea Catalogue.

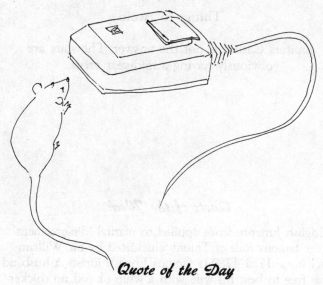

Quote of the Day

Passivity is the dragon that every woman has to murder in her quest for independence.

Jill Johnston

June 15–21

Gloria Steinem *Outrageous Acts and Everyday
Rebellions*

Advice for the Week

There is no advice or divination that will help you
through this week; Jupiter's Casino could be the
answer, but only if you travel alone and have unlimited
finances.

Things to Avoid

Jupiters Casino is not the answer. The stars are
obviously having a mid-year crisis.

Quote of the Week

English Jurisprudence applied to marital 'disagreement'
the famous *Rule of Thumb* elucidated by Sir William
Blackstone 1723–1780 (a famous English jurist): a husband
was free to beat his wife with a whip or rod no thicker
than his thumb, 'in order to enforce the salutary
restraints of domestic discipline'.

Barbara Walker

June 22, Winter Solstice

Book of the Week
Susan Brownmiller *Against Our Will*

Advice for the Day

This is the winter solstice. That means from now on
the days are getting longer and the nights are getting
shorter. Bad news for all housewives, good news for
the kids of course. It's hard to get the kids into bed
by 7pm, 'cos it's so light. If we were doing things
right, we would now be celebrating Christmas. But
then if we did that, how would you ever afford a
skiing holiday? Count your blessings on this
Solstice Eve.

Things to Avoid

Avoid pre-paid skiing holidays in Australia.

Quote of the Day

Envy, malice and all uncharitableness, these are the fruits
of a successful literary career for a woman.

Letitia Landon, 1836

June 23

Advice for the Day

There is no age limit for orgasms. You may have even
noticed the sly look of pleasure creeping across the
face of your ten month old as she fumbles inside her
Snugglers. Your mother is more relaxed and certainly
more beautiful since you gave her that vibrator for her
seventieth birthday. The secret? *Smegma*. Now isn't
that simply awful? That woman's orgasmic secretions
should be called *smegma*? Sounds like the waste matter
from an iron foundry. Start using the French term
jouissance.

Things to Avoid

Keep your vibrator out of reach of your toddlers.

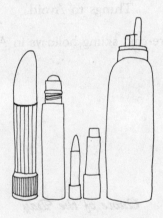

Quote of the Day

Now I know why I never had a Cosmic Orgasm. His
yang has gone sort of yuk.

Kathy Lette

June 24

Advice for the Day

And still on the subject of orgasms. Nowhere much will you find reference to the *quantity* of (grit your teeth) smegma you can expect, especially when you are into multiple orgasms. The range of M/Os is from 10 to 80 per session! A lot depends on your partner, your batteries or the strength of your wrists. And the quantity? Well, bucketsful my dear! There we've said it! Copious amounts, if you're doing it right. Open any medical book and you will nowhere find any reference as to where in your body you may be storing at least one litre of fluid that you can gladly release and not expire from the after effects. The mystery of the orgasm. Buy some towelling sheets. Compare notes with friends, even complete strangers warm to this subject. Remember if you're not getting it, you're not yet doing it right.

Woman's sexual pleasure, her orgasms, are for her pleasure alone, they are not related in any way to her reproductive cycle.

Things to Avoid

Avoid seeking any male advice on the matter—men are threatened enough as it is.

Quote of the Day

I've dreamt in my life dreams that have stayed with me ever after, and changed my ideas; they've gone through and through me, like wine through water, and altered the colour of my mind.

Emily Bronte

June 25

Advice for the Day

It's a good day to love your stretch marks, they are the sins, sorry, signs of your creativity after all! And stop saying that they are from making babies, they are from creating people! Let's face it, babies are not all that popular out there. I mean no one ever invites them to dinner parties do they?

Things to Avoid

Polyfilla does not help.

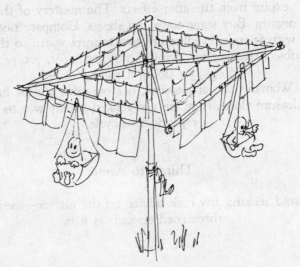

Quote of the Day

Considering how dangerous everything is nothing is frightening.

Gertrude Stein

June 26

Advice for the Day

Don't let your husband discourage you from going for
that university degree. Remember: man feels more
secure if he can denigrate woman's brain, it serves
them better for us to be kept ignorant otherwise we
might find out just how stupid *they* really are. That's
why they don't televise Parliament.

Things to Avoid

Avoid believing in male logic.

Quote of the Day

Men have had every advantage of us in telling their own
story. Education has been theirs in so much higher a
degree; the pen has been in their hands.

Jane Austen

June 27

Advice for the Day

Time to take stock today. Stocktaking Day!
Among other things count and sort out:
- The endless numbers of tabasco sauce bottles you have in the cupboard and ask yourself why you even bought one, let alone another 6;
- The numerous jars of Vegemite that are not quite empty;
- Find all those hundreds of rolls of cellotape that you can never find.

Things to Avoid

Avoid the temptation of trying to find the end of the cellotape rolls.

Quote of the Day

My mother always told me I would never get married because I liked being with my chums too much.

Dorothy Balmer

June 28

Advice for the Day

Graffiti Day today. Always venture into the city armed
with a large black felt pen in your bag and whenever
you are in those toilets that have Rentokil Bins in
them you must write boldly on the lid: 'Menstruation
is NOT a job for Rentokil!', 'Menstruation is NOT
unhygienic'. Let's face it, Rentokil makes you feel as
though you have a cockroach 'problem' instead of a
normal bodily function.

Things to Avoid

Not the day to feel unprotected. After all women are
not threatened by menstruation and if we don't need
protection from it who does? Hmmm?

Quote of the Day

The word hysteria was coined by some old Renaissance
doctor to describe 'women's problems', which occurred
because he thought her womb sometimes became
detached from its place and wandered about inside her
body—isn't that hysterical! My friend Dale Spender says
that if women get hysterical, then men get penisolent.

Gemma Hatchback

June 29

Olive Schreiner *The Story of an African Farm*

Advice for the Day

Your creativity will positively peak around mid-morning. Don't let it go to waste. Get up at 4am and start at once! Macramé old sheets together to make a trellis for the choko vines. Glue dead matches together to make the logs for the winter fires, make maxi-skirts from old egg cartons . . . the possibilities are endless. Let your imagination run wild.

Things to Avoid

Not a good day to contemplate joining the CWA.

Quote of the Day

My husband and I have figured out a really good system about the housework: neither one of us does it.

Dottie Archibald

June 30

The Cow

The next time you hear that expression 'old cow' wonder at the purpose behind its denigration. 'The cow was the totemic image of the Great Goddess. The animal herself served as wetnurse to the human race. Cattle were first domesticated in order that people might feed themselves and their children on cows' milk. In Egypt Isis-Hathor was the divine cow (kau) whose udder produced the Milky Way and all the stars. In Greece the white Cow-goddess was called Io, the Moon. The name of the biblical matriarch Leah also means 'wild cow', a title of the Mesopotamian Goddess. In India the Goddess has always been the sacred cow 'fountain of milk and curds'.

Barbara Walker

Quote of the Day

To live several lives, you have to die several deaths.

Françoise Giroud

July 1

'Being a working mother' (what a ridiculous phrase, every mother is a working mother, it's being a *paid* mother that we're talking about). Being a paid-for-working-mother does have its advantages. Money is probably the biggest one, but it does mean that your six year old will have to learn to cook. Keep giving him Christmas presents like Margaret Fulton's *Complete Home Cooking* and Adele Davis' *Let's Cook It Right.*

Things to Avoid

Avoid *The Macrobiotics Cookbook*. The products are expensive and you will be using up all your lunch hour driving round to obscure healthfood shops finding the right ingredients.

Quote of the Day

Currer Bell, George Eliot, George Sand .. did homage to the convention, which if not implanted by the other sex, was liberally encouraged by them that publicity in women is detestable. Anonymity runs in their blood.

Virginia Woolf

July 2

Advice for the Day

A day to become aware of the power that's been removed from our language. The word today is *gossip*, meaning women's talk, irrelevant, usually untrue. Originally it was associated with old wise women talking together. Probably they were sharing herbal remedies, healing potions, spells against incest, assessing the laws of the land and scheming to take over! Much the same as we do when we get together with the girls.

Things to Avoid

Avoid using the word 'gossip' for what men do. It's definitely one of *our* words. Reclaim its power immediately.

Quote of the Day

The original word was *godsib*, 'one related to the gods' i.e. a godmother—a term of respect. In pre-Christian times, elder women were considered divine because they retained their 'wise blood' after menopause.

Barbara Walker

July 3

Advice for the Day

Being a paid-for-working-mother means you not only
develop your third eye but you have to develop
alarm-clock-consciousness. On a higher plane this
would mean that you were in touch with the rhythms
of the planets but at the moment, on your rather low
plane, all you need it for is rosters. As you race around
to creches, friends' houses, after-school-care halls and
police stations gathering up your brood, be thankful
for your third eye and replace the battery regularly.

Things to Avoid

Avoid picking up the wrong children.

Quote of the Day

You are what is female, you shall be called Eve and what
is masculine shall be called God. And from your name
Eve we shall take the word Evil and from God's the word
good. Now you understand patriarchal morality.

Judy Grahn

July 4

Advice for the Day

When your mother said you needed something to fall back on she didn't mean a new sofa she meant your BRAIN. Take out your brain today. Give it an airing. Put it in the sun, clean it, nurture it. Ask it questions like 'What would *you* like to do?' Pay attention to it. If you neglect it, it could just go away from lack of love.

Things to Avoid

Avoid eating cream cakes. You need brain food. Try fish cakes, liver nuggets, carrot milkshakes etc.

Quote of the Day

I'm tough with my boyfriend. I give him blow jobs—with a hammer.

Sheila Shit

July 5

Advice for the Day

Time perhaps to join the workforce, get off the pension, sell the infant, make a break for independence, dust off your diploma, enrol for another one, start a women's studies course at the local playgroup, obtain a grant from community services, apply for a creative development grant from the Literature Board, borrow a video camera and make a really bizarre documentary about the things in your bedroom ... Look, the possibilities are endless, choose the one that seems the most difficult.

Things to Avoid

Avoid listening to your husband/lover but see what what the kids think, that's always interesting.

Quote of the Day

I would give up my life for my children, but not myself.

Kate Chopin, 1892

July 6–July 19

Mary Daly Gyn/Ecology

Your book of the week is *Gyn/Ecology* by Mary Daly. This is such an enormously important book and one that needs heaps of concentration you are advised to book into your local Travel Lodge Motel for *two weeks* to read it. Take plenty of Kleenex and bullets to bite on as you are going to get very, very angry. Remember to redirect your anger immediately into your fine sense of humour.

No **Almaniac** readings for two weeks will assist you in this most important of projects.

Quote of the Weeks

When women began wearing pants there was a tremendous backlash. I can remember—I was still practicing law at that time—going to court in pants and the judge remarking that I wasn't properly dressed like a lawyer. He's sitting there in a long black dress gathered at the yoke, and I said 'judge, if you won't talk about what I'm wearing, I won't talk about what you're wearing', because it occurred to me that a judge in a skirt telling me not to wear pants was just a little bit ludicrous. It's interesting to speculate how it developed that in two of the most anti-feminist institutions, the church and the law court, the men are wearing the dresses.

Florynce Kennedy

July 20

Book of the Week

Barbara Walker *Women's Encyclopedia of Myths and Secrets*

Advice for the Day

Stocktaking Day today:

- Gather up all those loose tampons and arrange them nicely in the fruit bowl on the sideboard, with a sign saying 'take one';
- Try to make sense of all the playing cards lying around in drawers: this could lead to a productive couple of hours building a house of cards or practising 'Draw the Well Dry' so you can beat your five year old tomorrow;
- With the help of a large magnet you can detect and gather together all your dressmaking pins and needles, razor blades and dead mice who have swallowed nails. Just leave them on the magnet.

Things to Avoid

Not advisable to watch Playschool today.

Quote of the Day

Any woman who still thinks marriage is a fifty/fifty proposition is only proving that she doesn't understand either men or percentages.

Florynce Kennedy

July 21

Advice for the Day

Old school friends will reappear in your life insisting that you don't look any different! Hard to believe when they look absolutely ghastly. Spend as little time as possible with them. Refuse all offers of luncheons on the grounds that you are a vegan or are on intravenous food support systems at the moment due to an unmentionable disease you were given by your third husband etc. etc . . .

Things to Avoid

Avoid giving out your real phone number. If pressed to give it, just make sure that the last digit is wrong.

Quote of the Day

Since when do you have to agree with people to defend them from injustice?

Lillian Hellman

July 22

Advice for the Day

Today in the train, plane or bus you may be
confronted with the Corporate Male, easily recognised
by the uniform: collar and tie (efficiently cutting off the
brain from the emotions, the head from the heart),
grey or blue suit and the lap top PC or wads of paper.
Smile sweetly, lean over and in your deepest, sexiest
voice say 'Hello big boy, and what have you done for
the planet today?'

Things to Avoid

Avoid approaching Corporate Business Women. They're
heartbreaking and lost, especially when they turn
round and say 'What planet?'

Quote of the Day

How can you possibly get serious about a religion that is
based on the fact that man got his first erection from
eating an apple?

Gemma Hatchback

July 23

Advice for the Day

Your husband may be entering his mid-life crisis at any moment. With men this can last a whole lifetime. Be prepared to take flight. (Qantas or Garuda, it doesn't matter now.) Really, it's not worth hanging around a disintegrating male, it's an ugly sight at the best of times and this is not one of the best times. You will find that he will seek solace in the arms of a young nymphet. This is fine. Yet another sister will learn early enough about having a baby around the house before she actually gives birth. As the poets say: forewarned is not foreplay.

Things to Avoid

Don't waste any energy on guilt.

Quote of the Day

There are certain cases in which, if you can only learn to write poorly enough, you can make a great deal of money.

Flannery O'Connor

July 24

Advice for the Day

Time to redecorate. Seagrass matting will hide a multitude of sins. Nail it to unsightly walls which have been disfigured by squashed mozzies full of human blood, blowflies full of maggots and texta full of venom. Many happy hours can be spent untwining it and macraméing it into complete ceilings to cover cracks in plaster and old bits of spaghetti. You will be complimented on your unusual sense of design.

Things to Avoid

Avoid reading *Home Beautiful*, ever.

Quote of the Day

Mama died at sundown and changed a world. That is, the world which had been built out of her body and her heart.

Zora Neale Hurston

July 25

Advice for the Day

Looking at your body today you see that one of your breasts is still a little bigger than the other, or perhaps one of your breasts is a little smaller than the other. Is this because all men have different sized hands? or because all babies have different sized mouths? or could it just be that all women applaud imperfection? After all it's so human. Very female. There's nothing as boring as the perfection/mind set of the patriarchy.

Things to Avoid

Not a good idea to get embroiled in this sort of domestic pedantry.

Quote of the Day

I think a lot of men feel that they would lose face if they admitted how capable their wives are.

Jane Bryant

July 26

Advice for the Day

Time for big changes: you could now put your house
on the market and buy a caravan—for the kids. They
will love the idea. Put the van in the backyard.
Persuade them to spend all their time in it, a
permanent holiday! Do not take the caravan with you
when you move, or any of its contents.

Things to Avoid

Avoid telling anyone you are selling. Panic will set in
and there will be a glut on the market.

Quote of the Day

Some women marry houses.
It's another kind of skin; it has a heart,
a mouth, a liver and bowel movements.

Anne Sexton

July 27

Grace Paley *Later the Same Day*

Advice for the Day

Selling your house has become a wonderful idea and
the focus of your life. Enjoy keeping it clean, painting
it, fixing up all those dreadful little scars of domesticity
that you have lived with for years. If it doesn't sell,
don't worry, now at last you have an inside toilet.

Things to Avoid

Never go to auction.

Quote of the Day

Pure selfishness is the motive of men's desires to oppress
women. They want women to specialise in virtue. While
men are rolling round the world having murderous and
otherwise sinful adventures of an enjoyable nature, in
commerce, exploration or art, women are to stay at home
earning the promotion of the human race to a better
world.

Rebecca West

July 28

Advice for the Day

If your house is going to auction this weekend it
would be wise to remove yourself as far away as
possible. Leave friends and relatives to guard the rooms
and watch while complete strangers rifle through your
kitchen cupboards and comment on your choice of
Ikea furniture. Be careful who you choose to have
raise the bidding for you. They might be confused and
start bidding against the agent's dummy and you could
end up buying your own house, then how would you
cope with yet another mortgage?

Things to Avoid

Avoid signing any contracts with yourself.

Quote of the Day

One hesitates to bring a child into this world without
fixing it up a little. Paint a special room. Stop sexism.
Learn how to love . . . vow to be awake for the birth. To
believe in joy even in the midst of unbearable pain.

Alta

July 29

Advice for the Day

Now that football has started you will find it hard to avoid. TV is the first privilege you should voluntarily withdraw from yourself. Thursday and Friday are footy previews, Saturday is the Match, Sunday the post mortems begin, these continue throughout Monday and Tuesday and by Wednesday they're on to covering the court cases and predictions for the Big Game.

Things to Avoid

Avoid complaining about the lack of coverage given to women's sport.

Quote of the Day

Having been overwhelmed by men's leisure activities on the television screen I once suggested to a BBC producer that he might like to do some programs on women's leisure habits: after thinking about this for a few minutes he asked in a perplexed manner, 'What exactly would they be?'

Dale Spender

July 30

Advice for the Day

Football really has a death-like grip on the world around you. Newspapers are the next to go. You will be unable to pick up a newspaper for the next four months and understand one word. The headlines read 'Eels Destroy Magpies', etc. Unpronounceable names like Wally Lewis or Dieperdiedomenico scream out at you. Best to ignore the papers and revert to Phantom comics. The *Almaniac* guarantees you will fiind no mention of football in a Phantom comic.

Things to Avoid

Fight the temptation to read the *BRW*. There's nothing quite so unattractive as the corporate male in print.

Quote of the Day

The future is made of the same stuff as the present.

Simone Weil

July 31

Advice for the Day

A desire to create could almost drive you into the
hands of your local surgeon to have your tubes untied.
Resist. Anyway tubal ligation is usually pretty final—it
has to be. Can you imagine?
Husband: 'C'mon darl, the bed's getting cold.'
Wife: 'OK, OK, I'm just tying my tubes, they've
come undone again.'
Direct your creative urges into the garden.

Things to Avoid

Not a good day to start work on the ornamental lake.

Quote of the Day

Give me a dozen such heartbreaks if that would help me
to lose a couple of pounds.

Colette

August

The football season is well under way and in order for you to survive it, the Goddess recommends deep sleep therapy. Not at Chelmsford or any other accredited institution but in the loving surroundings of perhaps an old school chum's flat, whilst she has gone off to Perth to pursue a new lover. The fact that the new lover has got two kids and a husband does little to deter your friend, who has always had no trouble remaining true to the school motto: Play Up and Play the Game.

August is not a good time to remember the night your husband proposed.

Your weekly reading list however must not go unneglected. Here it is.

Reading list for the month of August

Alice Rossi   *The Feminist Papers*
Keri Hulme   *The Bone People*
Antonia White   *The Frost in May*
Toni Morrison   *Beloved*

Quote of the Month

This August I began to dream of drowning. The dying went on and on in waters as white and clear as the gin I drink each day at half-past five.

Anne Sexton

September 1

Elizabeth Robins *The Convert*

Advice for the Day

Your exhaustion is overwhelming and you feel it's time to get another job (as well as this one). The stars are propitious for this extension of your already stretched resources. Women can do anything! and usually have to. You will be rewarded for your efforts—your kids will see so little of you they'll forget who you are and start asking somebody else to cook their dinner and find their underwear. Your husband, if he's still there, will be so surprised to meet you in the hall he may become quite attentive, even romantic, *sexual*.

Things to Avoid

Avoid working in a fish factory—you don't want to overload your husband's sense of wonder.

Quote of the Day

Many people feel that it is acceptable to offer textbooks to girl students entitled *Man and His World*; I wonder how they would feel if we offered boys, for 15 years of schooling, textbooks on *Woman and Her World*.

Gail Shelston

September 2

Advice for the Day

Contraception is very important right now. You could
be pumping out eggs at an incredible rate. It's just
your body feeling threatened and wanting to express
it's capability, after all there are about 250 000 of the
little ovas in there all waiting for recognition! Check
your diaphragm for holes. A blowout in a tyre can take
twenty minutes to fix but a blowout in your diaphragm
takes twenty years!

Things to Avoid

Avoid getting too obsessed and involved with taking
the temperature of your mucous, you could miss out
on a good fuck.

Quote of the Day

The side effect of contraception is that it is a threat to
capitalism and society as we know it. It enables women to
have resources outside the influence of men.

Margaret Sanger

September 3

Advice for the Day

Today is a good day to plan that move into a room of your own—preferably a studio set up that has no kitchen, no bathroom, a silent phone number and a double futon in a room with no windows, assuring permanent darkness. Something along the lines of The Tardis would be perfect. Looks like an automatic washing machine on the outside, something no one in the house will ever go near, but on the inside, *wow*! A fully equipped condominium!

Things to Avoid

Avoid giving your real name to real estate agents—ever.

Quote of the Day

Amazons took the isle of Lesbos and made it one of their 'isles of women', a sacred colony dedicated to the worship of the female principle, as later Christian monasteries were dedicated to worship of the male. In the 6th century B.C., Lesbos was ruled by a group of women devoted to the service of Aphrodite and Artemis, and the practice of charis, 'grace', meaning music, art, dancing, poetry, philosophy and romantic 'Lesbian' love.

Barbara Walker

September 4

Time to get a new bra, the scorch marks on your old
one have finally worn through. Remember your breasts
may no longer assert themselves, even if you do. While
you're there, enjoy trying on French underwear,
camisoles, teddys, suspenders; ask the supervisor if they
do a line in crotchless knickers, then ask if you can
have it all on appro. These hard-working lingerie
saleswomen need a little lightness in their lives. Think
of it. Everytime someone mentions the word 'cup' they
immediately see pendulous boobs swaying before their
eyes.

Things to Avoid

Avoid His Bras for Her, and all nursing bras.

Quote of the Day

You may try—but you can never imagine, what it is to
have a man's force of genius in you, and yet to suffer that
slavery of being a girl.

George Eliot, 1847

September 5

Advice for the Day

Time to take advantage of that free offer on the toilet
paper package and enrol for a Personal Stress
Management course. Everyone and her dog are into
PSM, in fact that's not a bad idea. Take the dog along
too! Her problems have only increased since you had
her spayed. She's still expecting her estrus and it never
comes. Her little doggy calendar has got all these big
red rings around certain days. It's only when you find
yourself down on your hands and knees inside the
dog's kennel reading *its* calendar that you know you
need help.
PSM can also help you with PMT, PND, EST, and
SIN.

Things to Avoid

Not a good day to stress out about filling in enrolment
forms.

Quote of the Day

Women didn't occur in Australian history. Elizabeth
Macarthur was never given credit for starting the sheep
industry. Read Catharine Spence, where women in South
Australia did all the work while the men went to the
goldfields back in 1851, but they were never given credit
for it.

Dymphna Cusack

September 6

Advice for the Day

Little did you know when you got married and said 'I do' how much you'd have to! Just remember he also said 'he did' and it's time to remind him of the vows, *for better or worse*; yeah, he couldn't have done better and you couldn't have done worse!

Things to Avoid

Not a good day to dig up your wedding dress. Best to leave it buried.

Quote of the Day

I think 'feminine literature' is an organic, translated writing . . . translated from blackness, from darkness. Women have been in darkness for centuries. They don't know themselves or only poorly. And when women write they translate this darkness . . . Men don't translate.

Marguerite Duras

September 7

Advice for the Day

Getting tired and exhausted could lead to domestic disasters, like burning down the house 'cos you're smoking cigarettes in bed. Adopt the advice of one woman who was so frightened of fire in her bedroom she didn't butt out her fags, she *sucked* them out! Smoking is not good for you or your children, as we know, but we find it awfully hard to remember this while we can still seem to breathe OK.

Things to Avoid

Avoid drinking coffee, talking on the phone, being alone, writing a book, relaxing after sex. All these things are conducive to the need for oral stimulation.

Quote of the Day

Women's minds cannot grow to full stature, or touch the real springs of our power to alter reality, on a diet of masculine ideology . . . .

Adrienne Rich

September 8

Marks and de Courtivron *New French Feminisms*

Advice for the Day

A good day to give up smoking! You will have huge
encouragement to do so when the results of your chest
x-rays come back to you today. Those spots have
definitely been diagnosed as lung cancer. You can
breathe a sigh of relief. At last you have a tangible
reason to give up smoking!

Things to Avoid

Avoid returning to the MD, chemotherapy, the knife
etc. Choose instead to cure yourself. Read Louise Hay
and Ian Gawler and get into meditation. Remember it's
not the cigarette that kills you, it's the match that
lights it.

Quote of the Day

During the 1970s clitoral 'relocation'—termed *Love
Surgery*—entered some medical practices. An operation
involved vaginal reconstruction in order to make 'the
clitoris more accessible to direct penile stimulation'.

Gloria Steinem

September 9

Advice for the Day

Today the sun will rise but your cakes will not. So stay out of the kitchen and well away from Margaret Fulton. Attack the Sarah Lee in the freezer if the desire to eat muck is uncontrollable. If the need to bake overcomes you, sit out on the banana lounge for three hours.

Things to Avoid

Avoid that glazed look.

Quote of the Day

Put this down in capital letters, SELF-DEVELOPMENT IS A HIGHER DUTY THAN SELF-SACRIFICE. The thing which most militates against woman's self-development is self-sacrifice.

Elizabeth Cady Stanton, 1890

September 10

Advice for the Day

Midday soaps are a big lure all week: if you feel drawn to the television knob—don't resist, go with it. Soaps are best appreciated when you turn the sound off and practice your lip reading. There are only about four stock phrases anyway:

- 'Do you want to talk about it?'
- 'Have you told him you're pregnant?'
- 'Why won't you marry him, Stacey?'
- 'I've decided to leave town and I don't want her to know.'

Things to Avoid

Avoid watching ABC/TV Education.

Quote of the Day

The great originators of ideas were not dogmatic or inflexible. It's their followers who are such dogmatic and dreadful people. A new tyranny is born every time there's a great original thinker.

Doris Lessing

September 11

Advice for the Day

Today is a good day to tell your mother that you now understand her behaviour all those years ago. It's a good time for you both to start talking again—*with* not *at* each other.

Things to Avoid

If things are going really well don't bring up the subject of the father of your children: you could set yourselves right back to square one.

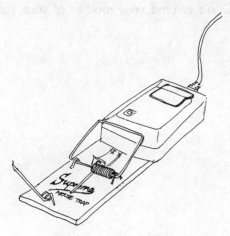

Quote of the Day

When I'm really old I'm going to become a Buddhist monk. I'm going to sit on a mountain in Nepal . . . no, Bali, it's warmer there, and I'm going to contemplate: whatever happened to my navel?

Gemma Hatchback

September 12

Advice for the Day

If it's your birthday today, send your mother a
congratulations card on having given birth to you all
those years ago. Remember what it was probably like
for her; women were never meant to be happily
pregnant, have orgasms or a paid job. And giving birth
to a daughter, well that was just 'bad luck'. No woman
ever forgets the fate of her mother.

Things to Avoid

Don't remind your mother of your age.

Quote of the Day

It's an odd feeling though, writing against the current;
difficult entirely to disregard the current. Yet of course
I shall.

Virginia Woolf

September 13

Advice for the Day

A good day to enjoy yourself. Perhaps a trip into town to sit outside the lawcourts and laugh at the sight of all those men milling round with little wigs on their heads that don't even fit properly, getting their feet caught up in their long black frocks and generally walking purposefully round in circles.

Things to Avoid

Avoid the temptation to expose yourself today.

Quote of the Day

If the millions of women who today are closely examining the reality of their situation, aspiring toward equality and wanting to live in a different way, were to become conscious of the responsibility of capitalist society for their present state, it would be an important step toward necessary change.

Madelaine Vincent

September 14

Advice for the Day

Another day to tickle your fancy and have a good laugh. Pop down to the local barracks where you will be thrown into paroxysms of laughter as you watch the Boys carrying their toys, all smart in their mix and match outfits. Observe them flinging their hands at their foreheads when they meet someone else who's got more jewellery on than they have.

Things to Avoid

Avoid the overwhelming desire to salute.

Quote of the Day

Woman's status as childbearer has been made into a fact of life. Terms like 'barren' or 'childless' have been used to negate any further identity. The term 'non-father' does not exist in any realm of social categories.

Adrienne Rich

September 15

Dale Spender *Man Made Language*

Advice for the Day

Time again to contemplate what it will be like when
the kids have gone, the husband's gone, the divorce is
through and the mortgage is paid off. Don't let the
terror of freedom overwhelm you. Just be grateful that:

- There are no more urine drips on the floor round
  the toilet;
- The flies stop hanging round the bed (why did they
  do that?);
- The dirty clothes are all yours and you can leave
  them where you like.

Things to Avoid

Avoid succumbing to your *nurturing* instinct and
opening your house to redundant executives whose
wives have replaced them with Apple Macintosh
computers.

Quote of the Day

Phallocentrism *is* . History has never produced, recorded
anything but that. Which does not mean that this form is
inevitable or natural. Phallocentrism is the enemy. Of
everyone. Men stand to lose by it, differently but as
seriously as women. And it is time to transform. To
invent the other history.

Hélène Cixous

September 16

Advice for the Day

Today will probably be a day of mourning—pet rabbits
expire in the heat, guinea pigs are eaten by the
neighbour's corgi, budgies escape through the holes in
the flywire, pet dogs are flattened by the neighbour's
Rolls (yes, we know you're living next to the Queen).
The list could be endless. Make the most of funeral
arrangements.

Things to Avoid

Avoid replacing anything immediately. Time is a great
heeler.

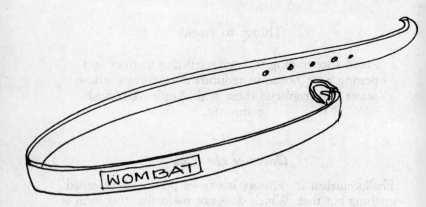

Quote of the Day

Society exists for man not man for society.

Emma Goldman

September 17

Advice for the Day

Today is a good day for starting a new family. A fairly
radical idea for some but not for you. Just inform your
present family, calmly and quietly, that you've done all
you can for them in the present circumstances and it's
time for you to move on.

Things to Avoid

Do not be dismayed by such words as 'Who else
would want you?'

Quote of the Day

They took our dollar note, they turned it into a coin,
and then they tried to float it! I mean any *child* could tell
you what was going to happen to it.

Gemma Hatchback

September 18

Advice for the Day

Time to plan ahead—if you are menopausal it's not too
late. Remember what the Goddess says: 'Menopausal
women are Wise women, they now retain their sacred
blood instead of shedding it. This means Big Taboo
and Power over Men.' All the money you now save not
buying overpriced insanity products can go towards
your akido, shiatsu, creativity seminars, creative writing
courses, etc.

Things to Avoid

Avoid reminding men that you have no use for semen
any more, as they will find you most unattractive since
they no longer have any power over you. Conversely
this could be a big plus, but remember, it doesn't mean
they won't stop raping you.

Quote of the Day

Let it not be said, whenever there is energy or creative
genius, 'She has a masculine mind'.

Margaret Fuller, 1847

September 19

Advice for the Day

Decide to put a little bit of magic into your marriage—
make your husband disappear! With bio-degradable
husbands this can be achieved by just leaving them out
in the sunlight for a couple of weeks.

Things to Avoid

Avoid marriage to non-bio-degradable men. Avoid
marriage.

Quote of the Day

Women, if you want to realize yourselves (for you are on
the brink of a devastating psychological upheaval) all your
pet illusions must be unmasked. The lies of centuries
have got to be discarded. Are you prepared for the
WRENCH?

Mina Loy

September 20

Advice for the Day

A day to contemplate—ironing. Most women are told,
as little girls, by their mothers: 'Never touch a hot
iron'. Unfortunately most women
forget this sound advice as they grow up. Take time to
remember that your mother was right.

Things to Avoid

Avoid buying clothes that have 'warm iron' printed on
them.

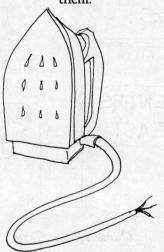

Quote of the Day

Did you ever notice how cancer-prone rats really are?
There's nothing you can give those buggers that they
don't get cancer from.

Ivy Bottini

September 21

Advice for the Day

Possibility of electric shocks from steam irons,
refrigerators or vacuum cleaners prove once again that
you should always wear gumboots inside the house.

Things to Avoid

Avoid your vibrator today, even batteries can be
over-charged at times.

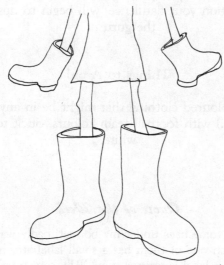

Quote of the Day

I am like a she wolf
I broke with the pack
I fled to the mountains
growing tired of the flatlands

Alfonsina Storni

September 22–29, Grand Final Week

Book of the Week

Jean Devanny *Point of Departure*

Advice for the Week

Time to book yourself into the ashram, just till Grand
Final is over. A course on advanced meditation, your
book, and lentil stew will ensure blissful hours, just
you and your farts. Be in the moment!
Avoid too many yoga niddras. Your snoring, not to
mention your flatulence, will begin to upset
the guru . . .

Things to Avoid

Any coloured clothing that might be in any way
associated with football team colours. Stick to pure
white.

Quote of the Week

There are some bees under my bonnet, badly wanting to
swarm. Each one of them has a small label attached to it,
and on that label is written a WORD; sometimes several
words; sometimes only a mark of punctuation. Allow me
to let them out, one by one, not at all after the nature of
a true swarm which may comprise some ten thousand
bees, as my bee-keeping friends tell me, in a great black
lump; but singly, each with a sting.

Vita Sackville-West

September 30

Eileen Caddy *Flight Into Freedom*

Advice for the Day

Vacuums will be a source of pleasure today. They'll
suck on anything, and they are a great learning tool.
How big is your living room? It's 12 inches longer than
your vacuum cord! Yes *inches*. Come on, how many of
you out there, right now, can hold up your hand and
show me 468 millimetres?

Things to Avoid

Never throw away your old imperial tape measures.
They come in handy when reading the **Almaniac.**

Quote of the Day

What an age we live in, where 'tis a miracle if in ten
couples that are married, two of them live so as not to
publish to the world that they cannot agree.

Dorothy Osborne, 1653

October 1

Advice for the Day

Tai Kwando, Akido and Magnum 44s are designed to help you fend off attackers, wife-beaters, you know who we mean. But there is another way. Buy *Spiral Dance* by Starhawk and *The Grandmother of Time* by Z. Budapest and start today on *magic*. All things are possible, as Z. says: 'magic is only what's between the ears . . .'

Things to Avoid

Avoid telling anyone anything—yet.

Quote of the Day

I am a warrior in the time of women warriors; the longing for justice is the sword I carry, the love of womankind my shield.

Sonia Johnson

October 2

Advice for the Day

A good day to stand for the Senate. Brings good fortune. Funny how one *stands* for the house and then spends the rest of one's time *sitting* in it. The Senate must have been invented by a male.

Things to Avoid

Avoid Party politics; don't go to any parties that have politicians at them.

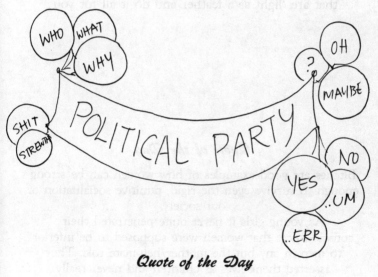

Quote of the Day

Went out last night
With a crowd of my friends
They must have been women
'Cause I don't like no men

'Ma' Rainey

October 3

Advice for the Day

Another day to contemplate—ironing. You know the
old adage 'Strike while the iron is hot'. It means
exactly that. Plug in the iron, call everyone's attention
to it and then announce that you are on strike. They
can do their own.

Things to Avoid

Do not succumb to TV advertisements about irons
that are 'light as a feather and do it all for you'.

Quote of the Day

Bitches are good examples of how women can be strong
enough to survive even the rigid, punitive socialization of
our society.
As young girls it never quite penetrated their
consciousness that women were supposed to be inferior
to men in any but the mother/helpmate role. They
asserted themselves as children and never really
internalized the slave style of wheedling and cajolery
which is called feminine. All Bitches refused, in mind and
spirit, to conform to the idea that there are limits on
what they could be and do.

Joreen, 'The Bitch Manifesto'

October 4

Advice for the Day

Sexual harassment will rear its ugly head today as you try to buy 'male' items like hammers, bullet head nails, circular saws, and nail bags—all of which you need for your home improvement schemes. You will be continually advised of your husband's needs and not your own. Assure the salesman that as soon as you've finished your period you will be quite capable of swinging the hammer. Demonstrate on his head if need be.

Things to Avoid

Avoid the 'know-all' approach. Strike a happy medium. When the equipment breaks down and you have to return it, you will find it easier to get replacements if you're remembered for your gentle manner. Ho hum.

Quote of the Day

What are these ceremonies and why should we take part in them? What are these professions and why should we make money out of them? Where in short is it leading us, the procession of the sons of educated men?

Virginia Woolf

October 5

Advice for the Day

Another day to contemplate—ironing. No ironing is necessary with today's fabrics. If you are quite happy with the crinkled look why shouldn't he be. Anyway you have long since given up looking at anyone before they leave the house of a morning. Why start now?

Things to Avoid

Avoid buying any clothes that do not have a little symbol of an iron on them with a big red cross through it.

Quote of the Day

She [Shug] say, My first step from the old white man was trees. Then air. Then birds. Then other people. But one day when I was sitting quiet and feeling like a motherless child, which I was, it come to me: that feeling of being part of everything, not separate at all. I knew that if I cut a tree my arm would bleed.

Alice Walker

October 6–10

Rachel Carson *Silent Spring*

Advice for the Days

A week to experiment with your personal eco-system.
A long-time advocate of live-and-let-grow, the Greening
of Australia begins right in your own bathroom.
Witness the mould you have been nurturing for years!
Now, encouraged by politicians of all dimensions, you
can go further! Start a no-dig garden—just toss all
those used Snugglers on to it. It will really stop you
wanting to dig in it.

Things to Avoid

Not a good time to start your baby on solids.

Quote for the Days

Can anyone believe it is possible to lay down such a
barrage of poisons on the surface of the earth without
making it unfit for all life? They would not be called
'insecticides', but 'biocides'.

Rachel Carson

October 11

Advice for the Day

More hints for conserving water will come to you
today from your higher self. Stop washing yourself!
The human body can go for up to six months before
it begins to flake off. Stop washing clothes! Just leave
them on the line for a couple of seasonal changes, rain
and sun will do the rest. Crusty knickers can be left
on ant's nests and overnight, those canny little workers
will munch away ... voilà!
In the morning—clean undies!

Things to Avoid

Avoid wearing edible undies.

Quote of the Day

Sometimes my Mother felt longings to be free,
but then a bitter wave rose to her eyes
and in the shadows she wept.
And all this, caustic, betrayed, chastised
all this in her soul she tightly kept,
I think that, without knowing, I have set it free.

Alfonsina Storni

October 12

Advice for the Day

Another day to save water. Disconnect the toilet and install a long drop. All it needs is a bit of sawdust, freely obtainable from your local sawmill (the money you spend on petrol will more than be matched by the savings on your water rates bill), and the odd dead rabbit. Composting toilets also seem to thrive on Annual Reports, K-Mart Catalogues, the *BRW*, *Playboy*, *Time Magazine* and all publications of Rupert Murdoch.

Things to Avoid

Not wise to put one of those trendy notices above the seat that says 'do not put anything into this toilet that has not been eaten first'—remember they have to wipe their bums.

Quote of the Day
Woman's work is always towards wholeness.

May Sarton

October 13

Starhawk *Dreaming the Dark*

Advice for the Day

Having thrown away all those expensive and destructive
cleaning agents you will only be using water for your
exquisite garden and bio-dynamic vegie patch (just
below the toilet) and for cups of tea. These are
probably also unnecessary as visitors will soon cease
to arrive.

Things to Avoid

Avoid going on talkback radio about this.

They call us militants, but General Westmoreland,
General Abrams, General Motors and General Dynamics,
they're the real militants. We don't even have a helicopter.

Florynce Kennedy

October 14

Advice for the Day

Domestic blindness or Vocal Slavery gets at you today:
  'Mum, where are my grey socks?'
  'In your room.'
  'Whereabouts in my room?'
  'In your wardrobe in the middle drawer where I put
  them, under your new underpants . . .'
  'Aw yeah . . . '
You see? You have just, verbally, walked into his room,
  opened the drawer and fetched them out. Don't let
  this happen any more. The best answer is 'I don't
    know' but if you're feeling playful you can say
  'Is my face red?'
  'No.'
  'Well, they're not up my bum then, are they?'

Things to Avoid

Avoid touching other people's clothes.

Quote of the Day

What strategy handed from ashamed mother to daughter,
what fear of losing love, home, desirability as a woman,
taught her, taught us all, to fake orgasm?

Adrienne Rich

October 15

Advice for the Day

It doesn't matter what star sign you are, today is an
excellent day for staying in the bath. Take a pile of
books, the thermos full of bancha tea, incense, candles,
cashew nuts, after dinner mints, whatever, lock the
door, disconnect the phone, take the kids to your
mother's . . . whatever. Then let H_2O take over. Pour in
the Lavender oil or Dorothy Hall's relaxing bath oil,
sprinkle rose geranium leaves or rose petals over the
water, pick out the aphids and you're away!

Things to Avoid

A photographic session. The prune look is not 'in' and
water plays havoc with cellulite.

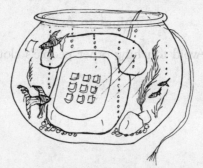

Quote of the Day

Politics is the reflex of the business and the industrial
world, whose mottoes are: to take is more blessed than to
give; one soiled hand washes the other; buy cheap and
sell dear.

Emma Goldman

October 16

Advice for the Day

A day of heavy bleeding could await you if it's your
time of the month. Wearing black underwear saves
having to buy Bio-Ad and polluting the environment.
The stains are still there but, as the poets say: if you
can't see it in this world then it exists in another.

Things to Avoid

Avoid shopping malls today, but if a bloodstain should
appear on the back of your dress in the middle of the
mall, hold your ground and announce defiantly, 'Well.
Look at that! Holy Blood! I bet it's the first *real* thing
that's happened here all week!'

Quote of the Day

A woman is only a woman but a good cigar is a smoke.

Rudyard Kipling

A man is only a man but a hot cup of tea is heaven.

Ingleton

October 17

Advice for the Day

Astral travel is on the agenda for today. The stars are
in alignment and you may be able to get right back to
where you started: young, a virgin, no mortgage, a
good job, a healthy body, no addictions, no in-laws and
a ticket to London flying BOAC.

Things to Avoid

Not a good idea to be out of your body if your mother
calls in or the children arrive home from school.

Quote of the Day

I'm Tough. If I get a flat tyre, I just let down the other
three and drive on!

Sheila Shit

October 18–24

Lynn Andrews *Medicine Woman*

Advice for the Week

Another week just flies by. On the wing, as it were,
focus your attention on the planet. How about a
protest at your local supermarket where you may stand
guard on all the products using CFCs or HFCs. Such
unnecessities as pressurepak underarm deodorant for
men. (Why don't they DIY their armpits? They could
just polyfilla up their pores.) Deter shoppers from
buying products made by the multi-nationals. Use any
means available to you. Refrain from using force until
you are out in the carpark, where you may freely
attack.

Things to Avoid

Avoid giving your correct name to anyone who may ask
for it.

Quote of the Week

After the first year husbands don't put the seat back
down any more. However there are compensating
advantages. I forget their names.

Barbara Holland

October 25

Advice for the Day

After your outrageous behaviour last week you may find that you are now barred from all your local supermarkets. This means a lot of travelling in the future as you drive the wastelands of suburbia trying to find a supermarket that doesn't have a life-size poster of you in the window saying: 'Beware Of This Woman'. Local street markets are safe and should be encouraged anyway.

Things to Avoid

False moustaches may work for men but not for you.

Quote of the Day

No woman can call herself free who does not control her own body. No woman can call herself free until she can choose, consciously, whether she will, or will not, become a mother.

Margaret Sanger

October 26

Advice for the Day

Force yourself to mobilise your family to take an interest in the Greenhouse effect. Let them know just how awful it's going to be. Install a sprinkler system in the living room, seal all windows and doors and turn up the central heating. Toss a few cane toads casually around as added decor.

Things to Avoid

Not a good time to lay a new carpet.

Quote of the Day

The freer that women become the freer men will be. Because when you enslave someone, you are enslaved.

Louise Nevelson

October 27

Advice for the Day

Get out and commune with nature. Visit a friend's
hobby farm. Indulge in all those fantasies you have
about getting away from it all. Watch her as she
casually gathers up the horseshit with her bare hands
and sprinkles it on her humungous vegie patch.
Observe her skill as she starts her ancient diesel
generator so that she may do a quick wash of the
mountain of unbelievably filthy garments that her
fourteen (they keep coming) children have piled up on
the verandah. Gaze casually at her fuel bills accounting
for the 1500 kilometers she has to drive every week to
get the kids to various extra-curricular activities. Go
home happy.

Things to Avoid

Not advisable to wear your new Reeboks.

Quote of the Day

Like abortion, the problem of violence concerns almost all
women, independently of their social class. It goes beyond
the frontiers of class. Women are beaten by husbands
who are judges or magistrates as well as workers.

Simone de Beauvoir

October 28

Book of the Week
Lynn Andrews *Jaguar Woman*

Advice for the Day

Another one of those days where supermarket trolleys
could undo all that wonderful work your Personal
Stress Management Course did for you last month. You
find yourself asking the age old question: 'If they can
put a man on the moon why can't they design a
supermarket trolley?' and you find yourself answering:
'If they can put one man on the moon why not all of
them?'

Things to Avoid

Avoid watching 'Beyond 2000'.

Quote of the Day
Oh, darling let your body in,
let it tie you in,
in comfort.
What I want to say, Linda,
is that women are born twice.

Anne Sexton

October 29

Advice for the Day

What is the secret of the happy housewife? Of having
that calm, sweet smile on your face all day as you slave
away? Of not getting angry with the kids or short
tempered with the moron, sorry, the husband? Light
up a joint straight after breakfast!

Things to Avoid

Avoid smoking before breakfast.

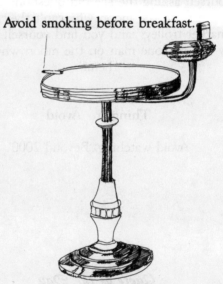

Quote of the Day

Men have committed the greatest crime against women,
they have led them to hate women, to be their own
enemies, to mobilize their immense strength against
themselves.

Hélène Cixous

October 30

Advice for the Day

If your husband is driving you crazy with such phrases
as: 'God, the least I expect when I come home from a
hard day at the office is a little peace and quiet!' and
you know that what he *really* means is: 'I have had
this really exciting day today, I met three new
marketing managers and they were really impressed
with me and I created a whole new porfolio for myself
and then I had to have lunch with this really
fascinating woman from 'Media Watch' and the girls in
the front office decided to spoil me like a child . . .
now, all I want is for you all to stop reminding me of
those committments I made so many years ago which I
now regret.'
Sit down and read Mary Daly, reminding yourself that
you have lifted the veil from that old argument and
tomorrow when he comes home he will find an empty
house. No you, no kids, no furniture. Nothin'.

Things to Avoid

Avoid reading, or believing Corinthians.

Quote of the Day

What is not a crime in men is scandalous and
unpardonable in women.

Mary Manley, 1696

October 31

Advice for the Day

The next time someone says 'your children are your greatest asset', ask your bank manager how much he'll give you if you leave the kids as collateral.

Things to Avoid

Don't fill out your income tax forms without sound advice from your accountant over this matter.

Quote of the Day

But when the children are away, when she is free, can sleep and wake when she wants, can sit, and sit, at breakfast-time, and tea-time, and supper-time, how young and gracious she can be.

Fay Weldon

November 1

Advice for the Day

Take advantage of the New Age Health Boom. Take
your first float. Sign up for 12 months of floating!
Float tanks are a wonderful way to release tension,
hide from the kids, relieve tired muscles, ease swollen
labia and empty full bladders ... oops, sorry, forget
that one. But remember Epsom salts are not good for
the sustenance of the bacterial environment of the
vagina—so be sure to stuff a handful of tampons up
before you get in.

Things to Avoid

Not a good time to remember your claustrophobia.

Quote of the Day

We are sort of airy clouds, whose lightning flash out one
way, and the thunder another.

Aphra Behn, 1680

November 2

Advice for the Day

A good time of the year to take up painting. The
weather is getting warmer, the days longer, the light is
perfect. Important to select the right sort of brush and
oils even if you are just a beginner. Choose your
subject with care—perhaps the front fence or even the
front door. The choice is yours!

Things to Avoid

Arts programs on television.

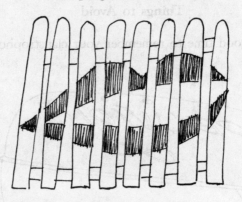

Quote of the Day

Modesty is masculine shame attributed to women for two
reasons: first, because man believes that woman is subject
to the same laws as himself; second, because the course
of human evolution has reversed the psychology of the
sexes, attributing to women the psychological results of
masculine sexuality . . .

Celine Renooz, 1898

November 3

Advice for the Day

The artist in you has finally awakened—having
practised on the house you may now move up to
canvas. The verandah blinds or perhaps the hammock?
You have centuries of styles with which to experiment
and subject matter galore. Primitives are popular—
perhaps the Country Practice logo? A religious subject
perhaps? The Holy Trinity: The Virgin, The Mother
and The Crone.

Things to Avoid

Don't succumb to criticism from your neighbours.

Things to Avoid

Quote of the Day

Unity in a movement situation is overrated. If you were
the Establishment, which would you rather see coming
through the door, five hundred mice or one lion?

Florynce Kennedy

November 4

Advice for the Day

A day to contemplate why it is that the male of the
species can sleep the sleep of the innocent, through
storm and rain, infant screams, electronic alarm
buzzers, early morning phone calls and pure physical
abuse? It is the Servant/Master syndrome. It's inbuilt,
it's genetic, it's a legacy of past lives and it gives you
the shits. Install castors on the children's beds. When
he is asleep wheel the children into your bedroom, put
the potty and a jug of water by the bed, lock the door
from the outside and go to the Hilton.

Things to Avoid

On second thoughts avoid leaving the potty or the
water by the bed.

Quote of the Day

Growing up white and male in this society is like
swimming in a salt lake—no matter how rotten you are,
it's impossible to sink to the bottom.

Sheila Tobias

November 5

Advice for the Day

Please to remember the fifth of November. Gunpowder, treason and plot.
You will notice today is not a day politicians like to remember, it makes them nervous. The possibility of planting a couple of crates of dynamite under Parliament House would probably have occurred to the average housewife before today but IF you did it today you would probably get off. For all Canberra residents the **Almaniac** highly recommends this adventure. If you can't get your hands on any dynamite a couple of bags of soiled nappies will have the required effect.

Things To Avoid

Don't let them take any of your good furniture for a bonfire.

Quote of the Day

Time wounds all heels.

Jane Ace

November 6

Advice for the Day

One of those days when you regret not having become
a plumber, instead of an Architect. Your B.Arch. will
not help you one bit when there's a dead frog stuck
halfway up the hotwater system.

Things to Avoid

Not a good day to watch David Attenborough's 'Living
Planet', especially when everything you seem to
encounter is dead.

Quote of the Day

Men are like old kings who think they are still in power
when they have ceased to reign.

Marguerite Duras

November 7

The Menstrual Calendar

The lunar calendar (Goddess-given menstrual calendar),
gave thirteen months to the year instead of twelve
(Christian, solar calendar), marking new, waxing, full
and waning moon—sabbaths in the ancient form.

Thirteen lunar months gave 364 days per year
(13 x 28), with one extra day to make 365. Nursery
rhymes, fairy tales, witch charms, ballads and other
repositories of pagan tradition nearly always describe
the full annual cycle as 'a year and a day'. This explains
the pagan reverence for the number thirteen and the
Christian detestation of it.

Chinese women established a lunar calendar 3000 years
ago and the Great Mayan Calendar was also first based
on the menstrual cycles. Romans called the calculation
of time 'mensuration' i.e., knowledge of the menses.

For fear of disrupting the Goddess's transitions,
activities of some kinds were forbidden on the seventh
day of each lunar phase; thus sabbaths became
'unlucky' or taboo. Because it was a time-honoured
custom, even the biblical God was forced to rest on
the seventh day.

Barbara Walker

Disinformation
Number thirteen is bad luck.

Quote of the Day

Lilly, promise me that my gravestone will carry only these
words: If you can read this you've come too close.

Dorothy Parker to Lillian Hellman

November 8

Advice for the Day

If the fact that every time your mother arrives for a
visit she is wearing rubber gloves and carrying
disinfectant upsets you, it's time to reassess how well
you want to get on with her in your old age. You can
completely sever all ties (not advisable) by screaming
hysterically that if you're a slut it's because she taught
you everything you know, or, you can smile gratefully
when she appears and ask her would she do the toilet
first, then the fridge and the shower last as even
though it's 2pm you haven't had time to ablute yet.

Things to Avoid

Don't ask her to do windows.

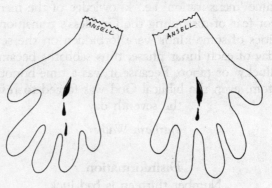

Quote of the Day

A woman
who loves a woman
is forever young.

Anne Sexton

November 9

Advice for the Day

When your mother said you needed something to fall
back on she was not wrong. A sense of collapse will
invade you today. Go with it. If you haven't already
bought yourself a comfortable sofa do so immediately.
Most women have chosen to fall back on a man, a
most unreliable form of support, far better to organise
to have a woman in back of you nowadays.

Things to Avoid

Avoid using men as sofas, they are far better as
hearthrugs.

Quote of the Day

If ants are such busy workers how come they find time to
go to all the picnics?

Marie Dressier

November 10

Advice for the Day

A lucky day for heights suggests more roofwork.
Cleaning gutters, replacing sheets of corrugated iron
(perhaps they *should* be the rusty ones but not to
worry, whatever catches your eye, go with it). If there's
no broken tiles, smash a few and then replace them,
reposition the TV antennae, add another course to the
chimney; simple little chores that will just roll off your
fingertips.

Things to Avoid

Avoid rolling off the roof.

November 11

Marguerite Duras *The Ravishing of Lol Stein*

Advice for the Day

This is the eleventh day of the eleventh month and at
the eleventh hour you are meant to stop whatever you
are involved in and '*remember*', for men, all those
terrible things they keep doing to themselves and our
children. It is time to break the chains that bind us to
their values. Men do have an obsession for
measurement, whether it be years, hours or inches.
Refuse to recognise Death/Marcations!

Things to Avoid

Avoid being at home alone. Get out and make this a
public statement.

Quote of the Day

In order to be the sort of woman who can live with a
man you become the sort of woman that no man wants
to live with.

Gemma Hatchback

November 12

Advice for the Day

A good day to repair everything below knee height around the home. This doesn't mean you should grovel or genuflect all day, take care of yourself! Pump up a lilo, put it on the skateboard and push yourself around the trouble spots singing excerpts from 'Porgy and Bess'.

Things to Avoid

Not wise to hit the high notes of 'Summertime'; your head could connect with the underside of the piano.

Quote of the Day

No more alternatives. Suddenly
now
you can see my small bag of
eternity
pattern of power
my ace my adventure
my sweet smelling atom
my planet, my grain of
miraculous dust
My green leaf, my feather
my lily my lark
look at her, angels—
this is my daughter.

Lauris Edmond

November 13

Advice for the Day

On the track of personal satisfaction, collagen treatments of the inner and outer labia have proven very successful for women wanting that 24-hour-a-day clitoral stimulation. Shoving unshelled macadamia nuts into the crotch of your undies will also do the trick. Some varieties of His Pants for Her come packaged with nuts already in them. Forewarned is forearmed but not necessarily foreplay.

Things to Avoid

One should really avoid all underwear that has anything written on it.

Quote of the Day

Women whose identity depends more on their outsides than their insides become dangerous when they begin to age. Because I have work I care about it's possible that I may be less difficult to get along with when the double chins start to form.

Gloria Steinem

November 14

Advice for the Day

Time today to book your children in for rebirthing sometime in the next ten years. Rebirthing centres, like private schools, have a waiting list well into the next millenium.
Warning: Rebirthing does not mean you have to get them back up inside you.

Things to Avoid

Avoid all downpayments on futures.

Quote of the Day

We met an old concubine in Shanghai. When the liberation came the Government said that concubines could leave. The wife and the concubine had lived together for so long that they loved each other, and the husband was such a . . . well, there is an Australian word for it, that they threw him out. I thought it was lovely.

Dymphna Cusack

November 15

Advice for the Day

Configurations of Saturn and Jupiter mean that you
will have an insatiable desire to eat your children.
Don't panic. Just observe how your mind works under
pressure from the cosmos. Chain yourself to the
kitchen sink (so what else is new?) to avoid disaster.

Things to Avoid

Avoid eating your children if possible; if not, make
sure you use plenty of garlic.

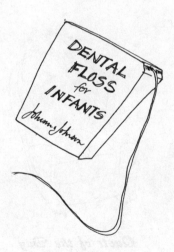

Quote of the Day

I got married and nine months and three minutes later I
had a baby.

Jayne Mansfield

November 16

Advice for the Day

Today you may happily transmogrify into an armchair.
If one more person sits on you, climbs up you, spills
their drink on you, vomits on you . . . you will have
permission from your higher self to transform—
immediately!

Things to Avoid

Avoid succumbing to looking like something out of the
Homesavers' Catalogue, or a Jason Rocker.

Quote of the Day

What's terrible is to pretend that the second-rate is
first-rate. To pretend that you don't need love when you
do; or you like your work when you know quite well you
are capable of better.

Doris Lessing

November 17

Advice for the Day

What starts today as a simple idea of cutting down a dress could lead to the dismemberment of your entire wardrobe. This is not such a bad idea. Plead domestic insanity and dump the shredded clothes in the Sallies' bag and go out to your nearest St Vincent de Paul's and replace them all immediately. You will feel heaps better.

Things to Avoid

Avoid the Salvation Army Stores for fear of being attracted to the same old rags you just got rid of.

Quote of the Day

A bad husband is far worse than no husband.

Margaret Cavendish, 1664

November 18

Advice for the Day

Today you will have a drug-free day. The stars are in alignment and you will able to cope all day on just hot water and a little honey. Trust me says your higher self.

Things to Avoid

Conversations with your higher self in front of the children or your husband.

Quote of the Day

The only way women can view their sexuality in our society is through the eyes of men. What's the alternative to a phallic symbol? I don't know. Men have never made one up.

Dale Spender

November 19

Advice for the Day

Time to do something concrete (an unfortunate choice
of word) to save the environment. Now that wholemeal
toilet paper has been invented how about inventing
wholemeal newspapers. Not only could you now wrap
fish and chips in them but you could eat the paper at
the end of the meal.

Things to Avoid

Not advisable to apply for a government grant.

Quote of the Day

Knowledge is power if you know it about the right
person.

Ethel Mumford

November 20

Advice for the Day

Pre-menstrual tension will affect you for most of the day whether your period is due within the next hour or the next three weeks. PMT can strike a woman down at a hundred metres, just be on your toes and have a pot of blackberry tea and a kilo of Vitamin B Complex ready to hand. Wear your 'STAY AWAY FROM ME, MY HORMONES ARE ACTING UP' T-shirt.

Things to Avoid

Not a good time to commit murder unless your period really does arrive within two days.

Quote of the Day

A man is in general better pleased when he has a good dinner upon his table, than when his wife talks Greek.

Jonson

A woman is always better pleased when someone else cooks the dinner thus allowing her to read Sappho.

Ingleton

November 21

Advice for the Day

A return to old fashioned standards. Take up knitting socks for the troops and hope they have a war soon in Antarctica where they will be fully appreciated. Maybe you could even knit sheep together, thereby cutting out the middle man.

Things to Avoid

Avoid singing war songs whilst knitting, e.g. 'An army marches on its stomach which is why the grub's no good; they desperately want them to get back on their feet and take their minds off food!'

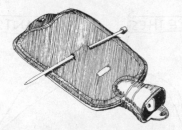

Quote of the Day

The eternal woman and the eternal limp prick. *That* was the basic inequity which could never be righted: not that the male had a wonderful added attraction called a penis, but that the female had a wonderful all-weather cunt. Neither storm nor sleet nor dark of night could faze it. It was always there, always ready. Quite terrifying, when you think about it. No wonder men hated women. No wonder they invented the myth of female inadequacy.

Erica Jong

November 22

Advice for the Day

Small things are set to jolt you out of your domestic torpor today. Funnel web spiders in the Bio Ad, cane toads in the self-raising flour, 24 000 volts through the electric toothbrush, razor blades in the pin box . . . just little things. So be attentive to detail.

Things to Avoid

Not a good day to walk around the house with the His for Her undies on your head—you could lose your sense of direction.

WHOSE PANTS ARE THESE

SHE PANTS FOR HIM

Quote of the Day

The female principle is an agent of transformation: she is both creator and destroyer. Hatred of the female principle stems from a fear of death. When we come to realise that death is only transformation, not an end, it will no longer hold any fear.

Diane Mariechild

November 23

Advice for the Day

Today is a good day to try on all your clothes, especially the ones you haven't worn for over twelve months. If the silver fish, moths, your body, your daughter's body, the Queen, Princess Di, Fergie et al have not made them redundant you may keep them.

Things to Avoid

Avoid keeping all clothes of brown, beige or orange tonings.

Quote of the Day

Women are from their very infancy, debarred those advantages of education with the want of which they are afterward reproached, and nursed up in those vices with which hereafter he upbraided them. So partial are men as to expect bricks when they afford no straw.

Mary Astell, 1694

November 24

Advice for the Day

A good day to tell your boss to get stuffed.
Don't expect to find re-employment straight away.
Never mind. A leap into the void is always
unpredictable but remember, fear is the greatest
motivator for change—just so long as you are prepared
to confront it. Not much money is to be made in the
void however. Here's a thought. Become a
Hygienic-Waste Recycler. All those rich people who
can't be bothered separating their garbage can hire you
to do it. You ease their consciences and earn big
bucks. People pay a *lot* to ease their conscience
nowadays.

Things to Avoid

Don't go on Midday TV Shows until you have got
your little empire totally set up. This idea will be
ripped off.

Quote of the Day

I should like to know what is the proper function of
women, if it is not to make reasons for husbands to stay
home, and still stronger reasons for bachelors to go out.

George Eliot

November 25

Book of the Week

Mary Daly Websters' First New Intergalactic Wickedary

Advice for the Day

Today is the perfect day to start a mid-life crisis—let's
face it—no matter what age you are you are always in
the middle of your life and a crisis is a nice way to
take stock.

Things to Avoid

Avoid ingesting paracetamol in large quantities.

 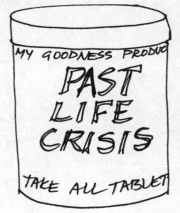

Quote of the Day

One half of the world cannot understand the pleasures of
the other.

Jane Austen

November 26

Advice for the Day

Health problems associated with your reproductive system can send you running to the medical profession today. This time take a copy of *Gray's Anatomy*, which you have committed to memory, and a copy of Louise Hay's *How To Heal Your Life* and don't leave the medico's office until you have managed to reprogram his mind and he understands the connection between the spiritual and the physical body and where pain really comes from.

Things to Avoid

Avoid signing forms that are asking for your OK to do a biopsy report.

Quote of the Day

I am reminded that a great compliment of my childhood was 'She's such a quiet girl.'

Michelle Cliff

November 27

Advice for the Day

MSG, CFC, HFC, 245T ... our language is becoming
a barrier to our understanding. Time to take note of
the naming/numbing reversal effect the mind-benders'
use of language has on the reality of their poisons.
Immediately procure a copy of *The Buyers Guide* and
cease to support the multinationals. Write letters to
them telling them to POQ with their SNAFU
mentality and to RIP themselves instead of our Third
World families.

Things to Avoid

Avoid procrastination ...

Quote of the Day

I've been poor and I've been rich. Rich is better.

Sophie Tucker

November 28

Advice for the Day

Another day to potter around your house, attending to all those DIY jobs. Remember DIY stands for Don't Injure Yourself.

Things to Avoid

Today will be pain free if you stay in the bedroom.

Quote of the Day

I know that when I write there is something inside me which stops functioning, something that becomes silent. I let something take over inside me that probably flows from my femininity. But everything shuts off—the analytical way of thinking, inculcated by college, studies, reading, experience. It's as if I were returning to a wild country.

Marguerite Duras

November 29

Advice for the Day

Another day of having to listen to the mournful cries of 'Why can't I ever find a pair of socks that match in this house?' Just reply 'For the same reason that you can never find a pair of tits that match outside this house'. It doesn't really make sense but he will ponder it for hours.
Get the jump on him tomorrow and say 'Why can't I ever find a pair of undies that match in this house?'

Things to Avoid

Avoid getting too embroiled in this sort of domestic madness.

Quote of the Day

In the Victorian era, leading authorities like Dr Isaac Brown Baker performed many clitoridectomies to cure women's nervousness, hysteria, catalepsy, insanity, female dementia, and other catchwords for symptoms of sexual frustration.

Barbara Walker

November 30

Advice for the Day

You have realised you are in a rut (remember the only difference between a rut and a grave is the depth). Immediate steps can be taken to alleviate/elevate yourself:

- Wear platform shoes, you will be able to see over the edge and they will match the rest of your outdated wardrobe;
- Dye your hair the opposite colour on the spectrum;
- Have a nervous breakdown.

Things to Avoid

Avoid writing letters to the editor.

Quote of the Day

Woman's status as childbearer has been made into a fact of life. Terms like 'barren' or 'childless' have been used to negate any further identity. The term 'non-father' does not exist in any realm of social categories.

Adrienne Rich

December 1

Ever stopped to wonder why we spray fake snow on a
fir tree and stick reindeer on the mantelpiece, sitting
down to stare at a jolly fat man dressed for an arctic
winter on placemats which await roast turkey and hot
plum pudding . . . when it's 32 degrees
centigrade outside?
It's really got very little to do with Christmas; it's to
do with the fact that we are indulging in the Winter
Solstice Celebrations (that dreadful pagan passion for
wine, yule logs and merrymaking) when in fact we
should be celebrating the Summer Solstice (more wine,
loaves of fresh bread and merrymaking).
This face-about is the result of our latitude. Ponder for
a moment the joys of being born into a mud hut in
Lapland. All of this would then make so much sense!
One would be positively grateful for the Queen's
Message if the temperature was 20 degrees below zero.

Disinformation

Christmas celebrates the birth of Jesus in 1 A.D. (Jesus'
birthdate wasn't decided until 400 A.D.)

Quote of the Day

Power is the ultimate aphrodisiac.

H. Kissinger

Power sucks.

Ingleton

December 2

Christina Stead *The Man Who Loved Children*

Advice for the Day

Only 23 shopping days till Christmas. It's good isn't it.
With the new trading laws, you can shop all week and
all weekend. Day and night. You can just shop and
shop and shop. You don't need money, in fact it's
preferable if you don't produce money over the
counter. Salesgirls nowadays give you a rather disdainful
look and put on white gloves before they'll handle the
filthy stuff. Try to achieve at least three different plastic
credit cards by December to impress the staff of David
Jones. Who knows, with any luck you may die before
January and you can leave all your credit cards to your
children in your will.

Things To Avoid.

Not a good time to spend any more money on other
people.

Quote of the Day

My mother is a poem I will never write.

Sharon Doubiago

December 3

Advice for the Day

Probably a good day to attend a wedding, even if you haven't been invited. Always remember, when attending a wedding it is possible to change the bride's mind. Try gentle persuasion, calm logic, blackmail or just lie. As a last resort when the minister says 'if there is any reason . . .' you can stand up and wave a piece of paper saying 'This man gave me herpes and if that's not enough he even gave them to my dog!' Ugly but effective.

Things to Avoid.

Not a good day for getting marred, sorry married. (When is it ever a good day to get married?)

Quote of the Day

For women interested in developing a deep humility, motherhood is an excellent training ground.

Mary Kay Blakely

December 4

Advice for the Day

Today is a day of real alternatives. Try drinking real
coffee as opposed to decaf and taste the difference! It's
amazing what a little caffeine can do for your day! Buy
a loaf of sliced white and taste the difference! You will
realise there is always free choice, you *can* choose the
way you want to die after all!

Things to Avoid

Not a good day to think of your candida.

Quote of the Day

Many years back
a woman of strong purpose
passed through this section
and everything else tried to follow.

Judy Grahn

December 5

Advice for the Day

A lucky day to cut hair. Your own or someone else's.
Any location. Armpits, legs, genitals, cats, dogs, the
flokati rug. Feel free to experiment. Save the clippings.
With hard times ahead you can use them for stuffing
pillows, knitting blankets and generally having a good
time when the power fails.

Things to Avoid

Avoid attacking the kid's Barbie Doll or Rainbow Brite.
You do irreparable damage to your plans for after-care
in your old age.

Quote of the Day

Our tongues are light because earnest in reproving
men's filthy vices ... and our fury dangerous, because
it will not bear with their knavish behaviours.

Jane Anger, 1589

December 6

Advice for the Day

Masturbation—not to be confused with mastication.
One means to chew your food, the other doesn't.
Masturbation, the bane of Victorian morality (but it
gave us great phrases like 'self-abuse'), looms large no
matter where you find yourself today. For propriety's
sake we hope you find yourself alone in the laundry
where there are all manner of exciting appliances to
help you in your endeavours. It is a well known
medical fact that migraines can be cured by a sensitive
bout of masturbation.

Things to Avoid

Don't ever use any electrical appliances whilst in the
bath.

Quote of the Day

The earliest Chinese ideograph for 'male' was also a
synonym for 'selfish'.

Barbara Walker

December 7

Advice for the Day

A lucky day for 'plucking' say the stars. Unclear as to
whether you should attack your face or the local
poultry market. Choose whichever seems to provide
the most possibility for personal satisfaction. This is
Golden Rule No 2. (Golden Rule No 1: She who has
the gold makes the rules.)

Things to Avoid

Avoid making any rules.

Quote of the Day

No one ever speaks of 'a beautiful old woman ... '

Simone de Beauvoir

December 8

Advice for the Day

Electrical repairs are not an impossibility: let's face it, if a man can learn to do it so can you. Just remember, the male plug goes into the female socket, red to red, black to black and the earth is green (why do men need to make it all seem so mystical and complicated?) Quantum physics, we assure you is just as simple. Start today!

Things to Avoid

Avoid touching metal unless you're wearing two pairs of Reeboks.

Quote of the Day

This book by any yet unread,
I leave for you when I am dead,
That being gone, here you may find
What was your living mother's mind.
Make use of what I leave in Love,
And God shall bless you from above.

Anne Bradstreet, 1650

December 9

Merlin Stone *When God Was A Woman*

Advice for the Day

Escape from home today at any cost. Driving is safe, especially if you stay on the footpath. You could even spend all day in the supermarket carpark, moving from one spot to another and having interesting confrontations with other shoppers as you steal their spots.

Things to Avoid

Stay away from Range Rovers and Volvo stationwagons; their karma is not good for you today.

Quote of the Day

How hard it is to make your thoughts look anything but imbecile fools when you paint them with ink on paper.

Olive Schreiner

December 10

Advice for the Day

A day for being on the roof ... 'when this old world
starts getting you down.' ... you know the song. Up
on a roof things become really clear:
- Why the TV aerial doesn't work;
- Why the water pours into the second bedroom;
- How the chemical reaction called 'rust' works;
- Where the top of your expensive stainless steel
  double boiler has been hiding all these years.

The **Almaniac** is not suggesting that you do anything
about these things, just observe. Meditate, take your
lunch up there, a carafe of wine, wave to neighbours,
be friendly, take your walkman and listen to Sting,
Aquamarine or Playschool tapes. Some women have
been known to spend days like this. Some women have
even been known to issue writs from their roofs.

Things to Avoid

Do not read *Fear of Flying* today ... and refuse all
offers of 'help' from men in uniform.

Quote of the Day

I cannot tell how Eternity seems. It sweeps around me
like a sea ... Thank you for remembering me.
Remembrance—mighty word.

Emily Dickinson

December 11

Advice for the Day

New Age Awareness suggests that this is a good time
for you to seriously consider changing the names of
your children. Cosmic references are fine, it's also
recommended to delve into the ancient mythology of
Greece, Egypt and Glen Iris. Try to avoid 'nature
orientated' names. They are now very passé.

Things to Avoid

Your children, who are strongly influenced by such
programs as 'Neighbours', will come forward with many
unpalatable suggestions. One of the big plusses of
parenthood is that *you* get to choose the name! It's
your inalienable right. When they are eighteen they
can do what they like. By then they probably won't be
on speaking terms with you anyway.

Quote of the Day

It's the things in your life that you refuse to acknowledge
are the things that will rule you.

Agnes Whistling Elk

December 12

Females are required to massage male egos—reflect
them at twice their normal size—for this is one of the
ways that the illusion of male mastery is maintained.
We don't show men up in public, we are trained to
pretend ignorance at male ineptitude, gloss over glaring
errors, change topics of conversation so that they may
appear at their most impressive and smile while
we do it.
There is an underworld of woman's meanings as they
make unspoken arrangements to rescue men out of
difficulty or disturbance. We perform these services so
often and the fact that they're not talked about, not
recognised as part of woman's daily reality probably
leads us to understand that if we assessed and
documented the enormous amount of unpaid, unfair
work involved in the task of emotionally managing
men they would STOP!
They might even start reflecting men at their normal
size and put an end to the illusion of male superiority.

Rebecca West

Quote of the Day

What you concentrate on increases.

Louise Hay

December 13

Advice for the Day

Things are hotting up on the Christmas Agenda. Time
to take that yearly trip into Myers to visit Santa.
Gather up as many toddlers as you can legally fit in
the stationwagon (it's possible to squeeze two into a
Safe'n Sound car seat if you take their nappies off
first). Strap them all together on a long leash and on
arrival at Santa's house, have an epileptic fit. It's time
Santa took some personal responsibility for all those
promises he makes.

Things to Avoid

Probably not a good idea to to do this if you are still
breastfeeding.

Quote of the Day

Giving birth is like having the biggest crap of your life!
The grapefruit up the bum right? And they make you
take it lying on your back with your feet tied up in the
air!

Bill Rawlings the pregnant man (AKA Sue Ingleton)

December 14

Advice for the Day

Could be one of those days when you are coerced into
having an 'internal examination' by an over-eager
medico, when all you are complaining about is a sore
throat. Most male medicos are keen to wreak havoc on
your personal power system. Remember the advice of
Sheila Shit: 'I'm tough with my gynaecologist.
Whenever he tries to do an internal I bear down and
as soon as he gets his hand in . . . I flex my perineal
muscles and break his wrist!'

Things to Avoid

Avoid going to doctors at all times. Iridology is the
answer.

Quote of the Day

Woman is not needed to do man's work. She is not
needed to think man's thoughts. She need not fear that
the masculine mind, almost universally dominant will fail
to take care of it's own. Woman must not accept. She
must challenge.

Margaret Sanger

December 15

Advice for the Day

Organising baby sitters is going to be a hassle today
and for most of this week really. This could be very
frustrating since there are all those fabulous invitations
to Christmas parties piling up on the fridge door. You
are going to have to be selective about which ones you
attend and which ones you can let go. Valuable criteria
for attending:

- Who will see you;
- Who you will see;
- Can they get you a part-time job;
- Is there anyone there who'd be interested in
  publishing your memoirs.

Things to Avoid

Christmas parties at your husband's office.

Quote of the Day

Men must learn to be silent. This is probably very painful
for them. To quell their theoretical voice, the exercise of
theoretical interpretation. They must watch themselves
carefully.

Marguerite Duras

December 16

Matilda Joselyn Gage *Woman, Church and State*

Advice for the Day

If it's Saturday, it'll be of one of those days when the cries of 'I'm bored' will drive you bananas. 'What's missing?' is the answer recommended by P.E.T. The easiest thing to do is to feign an attack of Alzheimers and just stare curiously at your children and ask 'Who are you?'

Things to Avoid

To be avoided at all costs: Parent Education Training handbooks and PGR on ABC TV. Somebody else's advice on bringing up your children only serves to make you avoid learning those lessons that you have come into this life to learn.

Quote of the Day

All pain is personal, it is between you and the thing that hurts. You may not be able to move the thing but you are moveable

Charlotte Perkins Gilman

December 17

Advice for the Day

Spend the day in the supermarket. The 'specials' will
give you minor orgasms and at this time of the year
any orgasm is a welcome reality.

Things to Avoid

Avoid buying any cleaning products that use a man to
sell them on TV.

Quote of the Day

Real men don't eat quiche, and real women don't eat
men.

Sue Ingleton

December 18–19

Advice for the Days

You are wondering if you are just suffering from
hangovers from all the office parties that you are going
to at this time or if you are suffering from morning
sickness. In all probability, since you haven't had a
period for six weeks this could be the case. Pregnant
for Christmas ... or menopausal? That is the question
and only the frogs know the answer. Get a DIY test
kit and put yourself out of your misery. Unfortunately
they don't have DIY scanners for menopause. They
don't have anything much for menopause except to tell
you that once again *your body is wrong*. and they have
pills and operations that can 'fix' you. Menopause, like
pregnancy is a natural event. Read the right books.

Things to Avoid

Avoid succumbing to the male mindset.

Quote of the Day

I'm not one for dance classes, feeling if God had wanted
us to wear leotards he would have painted us purple.

Victoria Wood

December 20

Advice for the Day

A good day to take the kids to the beach. Always a
very dangerous occupation if you are not used to being
on Red Alert. Being on Red Alert has got nothing to
do with communism or perestroika. It means you can't
read because, on the beach, your children are in
constant danger:

- That nice looking man is flashing his dick at your
  five year old. The fact that she is laughing is no
  reason to turn a blind eye;
- The boogie board that is tied to your child is
  slowly dragging him out and drowning him;
- That good looking surfer, whose body is absolutely
  fascinating you, is about to slice your eight year old
  in half.

Things to Avoid

It's a waste of time taking anything for your own
personal amusement. About the only personal thing
you can do on the beach is make shopping lists.

Quote of the Day

Mama exhorted her children at every opportunity to
'jump at de sun'. We might not land on the sun, but at
least we would get off the ground.

Zora Neale Hurston

December 21

This is truly a wonderful time, the spirit of Christmas is rife. Target and K-Mart stay open all night catering for those poor souls who wake up in bed at three in the morning remembering they haven't got a present for Aunty Eileen. At this time of year you can see people in their pyjamas wandering through the city in search of presents or just looking at the windows full of fairytale tableaus. Somehow no one seems to mind. Try it in the middle of June though and you'd be hauled off to the clink.

Things to Avoid

Do not let the children wear their duvets into town; they drag in the gutters and cannot be cleaned.

Quote of the Day

Bigamy is having one husband too many. Monogamy is the same.

Anonymous (a woman)

December 22

Advice for the Day

You have finished your shopping and you know that
they know where you've hidden the presents. You have
managed exceedingly well on your budget to buy all
those presents that they advertise on the TV including
$3000 computers for the kids and 'Kids! for Dad get
him this beautiful (!) $600 Black and Decker Chainsaw'.
Where do these merchants really think that a ten year
old kid is gonna get $600 for a present for Dad? From
Mum of course. Where would you be without those
Family Allowance cheques. Surprisingly there is still a
little of your inheritance left over. You're going to need
it . . .

Things to Avoid

Do not leave the house except in an emergency.

Quote of the Day

You know why the Pope don't hold no truck with that
IVF thing dontcha? I'll tell you . . . it's because the
chappie is putting his John Thomas into a test tube
instead of his wife and that means all those little Catholic
bubbies would be born without Original Sin! They'd be
Methodists or something . . .

Edith Wise

December 23

Advice for the Day

It's a good time of year to go through your drawers.
Get your passport out. (You do *have* your passport
don't you?) It's always advisable for a girl to have her
passport up to date. You may even come across that
Christmas card list that you made last January and
couldn't find this December. Life's like that: an
out-of-date Christmas card list.

Things to Avoid

Sending Christmas cards—ever.

Quote of the Day

One must not wage war on man. That is his way of
attaining value. Deny in order to affirm. Kill to love. One
must simply deflate his values with the needle of ridicule.

Annie Leclerc

December 24

Book of the Week

Jane Gardam *God on the Rocks*

Advice for the Day

Fly to Bali.

Things to Avoid

Avoid contact with any family and friends.

Quote of the Day

At work, you think of the children you've left at home.
At home, you think of the work you've left unfinished.
Such a struggle is unleashed within yourself, your heart
is rent.

Golda Meir

December 25, Christmas Day

Advice for the Day

A quiet day in the sun, drinking pina coladas and wondering why you are so happy. Your presents will be felt at home, not only felt but opened, most for the second time. That stash place was so obvious! Possibly good to ring home at some time and wish them all the best. Keep surfing.

Things to Avoid

Avoid all men on scooters with surfboards strapped to their ankles.

Quote of the Day

The scripture tells us that God created man in his own image, which has by no means proved a success.

Emma Goldman

December 26, Boxing Day

Advice for the Day

Ring your mother to assure her that you did not reveal
her new address to any of the family. Apart from that
one phone call you need do nothing. Go back to the
beach and don't forget the blockout.

Things to Avoid

Avoid succumbing to a Balinese Beach Massage. You
are going to need your legs when you get home.

Quote of the Day

We do not know what sort of society women would have
shaped, for their contribution has never been allowed.
Our cultural world is the product of male consciousness.

Dora Russell

December 27

Advice for the Day

Safe to return home. Relatives have forgotten you exist and everyone else has had time to go out and buy you the present they forgot to buy you. You will be welcomed back with open arms and empty stomachs. Not to worry! You produce a double jaffle iron that an extremely friendly young Balinese lad has given you as a going away present, and announce 'All our mealtimes are solved!'

Things to Avoid

Not a good day to put yourself forward as a leader.

Quote of the Day

They close in on me, pulling bits of my flesh and clothing for attention. One of these days I will come apart in their hands, and each child will have a little scrap of me to shout at.

Barbara Holland

December 28

Advice for the Day

In Bali you probably met some interesting people and always the most interesting people were 'In Therapy'. You are now far enough down the road of domestic insanity to warrant analysis. It's expensive and once you start you're there forever despite what the analyst will say at your first session. But it's the one thing you haven't tried yet, so go for it. It may even lead you into a new career option. Being a professional analysand! Try though you may to avoid it you will undergo 'transference' where you will want to have sex with your analyst (male/female it doesn't matter). This is normal. It is also normal to want to kill them. That is also OK. In fact you will find in analysis that *everything is OK*, which is why you keep going back ... for the weekly relief of being told this simple fact.

Things to Avoid

Do not share an analyst with anyone you know.

Quote of the Day

I don't know what a feminist is but I know people call me that whenever I express an opinion that differentiates me from a doormat.

Rebecca West

December 29

Advice for the Day

Today is the last day to eat ham, turkey, goose
leftovers. By tomorrow they will be rotten. Turn a deaf
ear to the cries of 'not turkey jaffles again' and smile
sweetly as you rub Nivea into your fading Balinese
suntan. Keep on letting them think you did something
'really awful' in Bali. It will keep their interest up in
you all of next year.

Things to Avoid

Do not feel guilty when you discover the frozen
blowflies at the bottom of the ham.

Quote of the Day

I wanted to wed the impossible
I wanted to wed what I wanted to be
I wanted to marry-o marry-o marry-o me.

Sue Held

December 30

Advice for the Day

A day of indecision. You could spend it in town
returning all the Christmas presents, the clothes/toys/
books that don't fit/work/interest you. You could just
spend the day in town buying yourself an outfit for the
New Year's Eve Party you've been invited to. You only
have one outfit and since the last time you wore it was
last New Year's Eve you could end up being very
depressed tomorrow night—not a pleasant thought.
Whatever you decide, you're going to have to take the
kids somewhere as their in-house behaviour is slowly
driving you to hard drugs.

Things to Avoid

Do not decide to run up a dress for tomorrow.

Quote of the Day

When a woman comes to write a novel, she will find that
she is perpetually wishing to alter established values—to
make serious what appears insignificant to a man, and
trivial what is to him important. For that she will be
criticised.

Virginia Woolf

December 31, New Year's Eve

Book of the Week

Dora Russell *The Tamarisk Tree*.

Advice for the Day

So here you are. You have made it to New Year's Eve.
A pity that your candida diet is going to prevent you
from imbibing tonight, but then someone has to stay
sober enough to drive home. If life seems a little
repetitive at times it's only because it is.
If you are one for making resolutions this is a good
time to do it. After the year you've just been through
perhaps a helpful resolution would be something along
these lines:
I swear to love, honour and obey myself, for better or
worse, in sickness (which I can cure myself) and in
health (which I can create myself), keeping myself true
to myself and forsaking all others for me. Till death do
us part, my body and me.

Things to Avoid

Doubt.

Quote of the Day

I'm a happily unmarried bisexual mother of two. No . . .
three! I've got two children by my ex-husband, one by my
lover and the next one I'll probably have by myself.

Gemma Hatchback